Lived Stories

Madhu Bhaduri retired from the IFS as Ambassador to Lisbon (Portugal) in 2003. After retirement, she joined the RTI campaign as an activist, and in 2012, became a founding member of the Aam Aadmi Party, which she was the first to leave within a year. Bhaduri has nurtured a lifelong appreciation of literature, philosophy, music, cuisine, and been a keen observer of paradoxes inherent in different cultures. She has published four novels in Hindi, one of which has been translated and published in Russian.

Lived Stories

Madhu Bhaduri

With a Foreword by
Aruna Roy

Orient BlackSwan

LIVED STORIES

ORIENT BLACKSWAN PRIVATE LIMITED

Registered Office
3-6-752 Himayatnagar, Hyderabad 500 029, Telangana, India
e-mail: centraloffice@orientblackswan.com

Other Offices
Bengaluru, Chennai, Guwahati, Hyderabad, Kolkata,
Mumbai, New Delhi, Noida, Patna, Visakhapatnam

© Orient Blackswan Private Limited 2021
First published by Orient Blackswan Private Limited 2021

ISBN 978-93-5442-082-5

Typeset in
Dante MT Std 11/13.5 *by*
Le Studio Graphique, Gurgaon 122 007

Printed in India at
Thomson Press, New Delhi 110 020

Published by
Orient Blackswan Private Limited
3-6-752 Himayatnagar, Hyderabad 500 029, Telangana, India
e-mail: info@orientblackswan.com

Contents

Foreword

These compelling stories weave together the thoughts of a writer and the complex demands of her diplomatic career. It is a story of a woman in a man's world—a committed worker in the mesh of politics and government control. These stories are fascinating for they satisfy the curiosity in all of us for whom a peep into human compulsions and the making of history has relevance and learning. Madhu Bhaduri's account in *Lived Stories*, without declaring it to be so, provides a woman's view as a distinct skein in the tapestry of diplomacy and government.

In 1968, Madhu qualified in the joint civil services examination and since she ranked high, she got her preference to join the Indian Foreign Service (IFS). In those days, it was still a coveted service. Today, I have heard that the ranking of preferences has turned turtle, with sometimes the Income Tax Service outstripping the others! This is an implicit comment on the nature of the Indian middle class—shifting from prestige and position to money. It is said that it is 'far more lucrative' to be collecting income tax than managing India's interests abroad! But the IFS also lost its shine as the nature of international diplomacy changed.

Foreign services and Ambassadors had their era till the 1960s. By the time independent countries matured in the mid-twentieth century and democratic mores were established, foreign affairs began to shift focus from Ambassadors to directives from State departments and External Affairs Ministries. This is true of India's diplomats abroad, as well as those who were sent to India in the days of strict Non-Alignment in a bi-polar Cold War world. The newly formed independent country had a series of extraordinary public intellectuals and statesmen appointed as Ambassadors to India— Chester Bowles, John Kenneth Galbraith, and a poet, Octavia Paz, who went on to win the Nobel Prize for literature, to name a few. But very few names stand out from the scores of Ambassadors who have lived in New Delhi over the last three to four decades.

Nevertheless, *Lived Stories* gives us an opportunity to understand how important it is to be a diplomat living in a different country to understand even today's world. The book records the perspective through the lens of a public servant determined to do her best, regardless of the glamour of the issue or the post. Like all good writers, she spins her stories within the complexity of ordinary and extraordinary lives, making facts state their case, with an emerging understanding of the mesh of socio-political and economic pulls. Madhu writes as Madhu is: straightforward, honest, and committed to the values she promised to protect.

She has been a friend in my personal life and a persona in the drama of my public action since the years we spent together in Indraprastha College (IP), Delhi. She was a senior who struck awe because of her straightforward expression and her courage to be who she was. She taught Philosophy in IP and I, a few years her junior, taught English for a year when we met and became friends. I saw great qualities in this slight, elegant woman whose 'mind is without fear'. As a younger person who admired these virtues, our friendship began with my admiration and her kindness. She was, she said, quite clear that a professional calling was critical for her well-being. I was brought up to believe that the traditional ambition of marriage was a limited canvas for women determined to exercise their intellect and intelligence. That shared view was a strong foundation which would last the rest of our lives.

The trajectory of our friendship (she became a member of the IFS and I, of the Indian Administrative Service [IAS], in 1968) remains strong, even while containing sharp differences, most notably over the 'Jan Lokpal' debates. We remain friends through the meanderings of a lifetime and to quote Rabindranath Tagore again, the 'narrow domestic walls' were broken by both of us, as they were built.

When I decided to leave the IAS in 1974–75, Madhu was on a posting to Delhi in the Ministry of External Affairs (MEA). I remember an evening in her beautiful home, rented from the well-known designer Riten Mozumdar, in Sarvodaya Enclave in Delhi. I went to meet Madhu, Amit, and a few other friends to tell them I had decided to quit the IAS. It was important for me to hear what she and Amit had to say. Their unstinting support further sealed my determination to quit. For both of us, the *'kursi'* was never important. In fact, retiring or resigning from the civil service spelt liberation.

From then, till the days of the Lokpal and after, we remained allies, communicating details and sharing concerns, although we were in such different spheres. For the most part, she remained on the fringes of my professional life in the early years, as I remained on the fringes of hers, as she was often on foreign postings and was busy moving from country to country. I have partially heard many of the stories in this book, and they have been a part of my cherished memories. I visited her in Vienna, where Madhu and the music were a heady combination, and in Lisbon, which was a cultural revelation for me. The reading of the narrative renews my relationship with Madhu, the intimacy of which is often lost in small talk in brief meetings. The writer rekindles my memory of Madhu the committed public servant, and of the affection and appreciation that lives on.

She wrote in Hindi initially and I was a recipient of her books, and sometimes she discussed them with me. She is a simple storyteller. Her strong voice, unwavering and searching for logic and justice in the messy existence of fellow beings, was always direct and persuasive. She is never didactic. She writes of the human condition, where faith in justice and a critique of its absence form the core.

Many of the stories in this book bring back a strong sense of nostalgia for principles now lost in political chaos, and sharp memories of a lasting friendship. For me, the political and the personal are embedded in every experience and act. These stories, as much as

Madhu's life itself, reflect those values. Her attempts to protest the ban by the Government of India on the showing of a film in Austria, and her involvement with the dubbing of a film into English in Vietnam are carefully recounted. Her recollections of her posting in Mexico mirror for me the excitement of the few meetings in that period and the occasional letters we exchanged. This was my first 'real' exposure to a culture that intrigued and fascinated me. The literature, the politics, and the differences between, if you like, 'oriental' and Latin American cultures were very interesting. In her recollections of Mexico, without going into a theoretical discussion on race and colour, Madhu tells us of Rakhi, her daughter, standing up to white racism and the extraordinary response of the driver of their school bus. More than any deliberative discourse, this small incident tells us of the courage of a young girl to fight back and the natural response of people who believe in equality.

The political cultures of Latin America, with its politics and great writers, act as a counterpoint to the texture of South Asian politics and cultural expression. The comparisons are echoed in these uncomplicated stories. Hamburg, Minsk, Lisboa, and every posting brought a different flavour to my life in rural Rajasthan. Her retelling of the Muthamma incident or of the plight of the illegal immigrants in Minsk has a continuing contemporary resonance. As we witness the COVID-19 migrant labour crisis and see migrant labourers being subjected to unequal hardships in their own country, the fate of the immigrant seems to be universally blighted.

I do hope she writes the rest of her 'lived stories'. These simply told tales have much to teach us. The message is straightforward. Power and privilege bring responsibility with them—to stand up to the morally deviant everywhere. They are reminders that evoke the fundamental onus of a representative of the government to adhere to these principles—of ethics and of the Constitution—a pledge we take when we enter the civil services.

Her stories are powerful because there is the directness of a 'tête-à-tête', an exclusive conversation between the writer and the reader. This will appeal to a wide range of readers, forever curious to know about what goes on behind the screen of governmental privilege. As they unfold, the anecdotes also guide those interested in ethical governance to pursue their own similar journeys. She seems to say that it is possible to sustain one's integrity so long as one can take the consequences of 'punishment' postings. Aspirants to the civil service, too, should be inspired by these tales to understand how constitutional values and processes can be used as operational tools in governance. After all, it is possible even today to stand with justice, for what is correct and fair.

Rajasthan, July 2021 **Aruna Roy**

Preface

The idea of writing about some of my experiences in the various places I was posted to during my time in the Indian Foreign Service (IFS) had been tugging at me for quite some time. Lethargy and just not getting down to it has delayed the exercise by some years. The list of my lived stories is long. Here, I have chosen to share those which have more than personal and momentary relevance. The 'left out' ones are valuable to me personally and will remain my private treasure.

Some of my friends wanted me to write these bundles of experiences in English because they do not read Hindi. I did think I would do that, but when the pen touched paper, it did so in Devnagari script, like reflex action, quite automatically. In deference to Ingrid, Kunda, Navrekha, and Sudha, I am rewriting the Hindi version in English.

Retirement from the IFS came with an enormous sense of having earned my 'liberation'. Not to be responsible to anyone but myself was like shaking off a heavy burden from my shoulders. It gave me a sense of lightness. In addition, freedom from 'representational duty' was most addictive. I vowed to make my post-retirement home without the paraphernalia of representation. National day receptions, formal dinners, and cocktail parties were deleted, once and for all.

Before joining the Foreign Service, I had been a lecturer in Philosophy at Indraprastha College in Delhi University. Those three teaching years had left an enduringly pleasant memory. Later, from time to time I had wondered if it was not a mistake to have switched from teaching to diplomacy.

This collection of my experiences almost wholly comprises memories of incidents in the places I was posted to during my career in the Foreign Service. I have added to these a few post-retirement adventures and misadventures. Some of these happenings have added a dimension to my understanding and others have drastically changed my perceptions and perspectives of people, places, and also of myself.

Lived Stories first appeared in instalments in *Hans*, the Hindi literary journal, in the form of a travelogue: *Safarnama*. It was entirely the encouragement of Professor Apoorvanand of the Hindi department of Delhi University, and the overwhelming response from the readers of *Hans* that resulted in this much longer English version. I am very grateful to them for motivating me to write this book.

1

Vienna, 1970

Two years after joining the Foreign Service and completing training in various fields, including district training for six months, I was allotted German as my compulsory foreign language and was posted to Vienna. A level of proficiency in the language allotted was a condition for confirmation in service. In those days of very limited foreign exchange, going abroad was not easy. A tourist was entitled to take not more than a paltry sum of US\$ 8 on setting out. Since it was so difficult, travelling abroad appeared more like a dream to every young man or woman. I remember watching a group of my college friends sitting around a pandit with their palms stretched out eagerly, waiting for answers to the two invariable questions, one of which was: 'When will I go abroad?'

What added to the excitement was the prospect of going to Vienna, the city which had once been the crown of the Austro-Hungarian Empire, the centre of music, philosophy, science, and mathematics, the home of towering intellectual personalities. What I did not know then, but was to gradually discover for myself, were Viennese coffee and an unmatched cuisine.

I was young and eager when I arrived at the South Railway station of Vienna after an overnight train journey from Rome. The historic city was glowing in the bright sunshine. My first task was to learn German. For this, I attended a course at Vienna University. My afternoons were spent in learning on-the-job consular work at the Embassy. My classmates in the German class took me for a typist when they heard that I was working at the Indian Embassy.

A woman diplomat was uncommon. It was almost unheard of. The most embarrassing was to be mistaken for the wife of my boss, the Ambassador. The American Ambassador would not stop calling me Mrs Trivedi.

I have a deep interest in classical music and was amazed at the enormous possibilities of hearing the world's best-known musicians. Music performances were highly subsidised by the government. I could buy a reasonably good ticket for the amount it cost to post a letter from Vienna to India. For students, it cost half of that. I recall an incident when Prime Minister Indira Gandhi visited Vienna in 1971. She toured several countries before the Bangladesh War of 1971 to draw the attention of world leaders to the genocide in East Pakistan and the unending flood of refugees pouring from there into India, which was an unprecedented burden and a humanitarian crisis the country could not manage without international support. Millions of people had already come and more were coming.

Before coming to Vienna, Mrs Gandhi had expressed her desire to hear Beethoven's opera *Fidelio*, a special performance of which was presented in Vienna's beautiful opera house. I had the privilege of attending this performance although I was a mere Third Secretary then. Today, such a thing would be unheard of. At an appropriate moment, I told the Prime Minister that the subsidy given by the Austrian government to just four of Vienna's music halls amounted to more than the entire budget of the Foreign Ministry of the country. She was surprised and expressed her amazement by saying, 'A very civilised country.'

A lot has changed since then. The meaning of 'civilised' is not the same, nor is the price of tickets for music performances in today's Vienna.

The visit of the Indian Prime Minister was followed by a series of happenings in the subcontinent, including the war in 1971 which created conditions for the birth of Bangladesh, a new nation. The image of a Gandhian nonviolent India was shattered. Its place was taken by a new image of an India which called itself Non-Aligned, but when convenient, did not stop short at drawing close to the Soviet Union. Newspapers and TV channels carried much that was considered 'negative', and caused a storm in the Ministry of External Affairs (MEA) in Delhi and Indian missions abroad. All Indian missions were struggling to prevent the soiled image from getting worse. Around this time, I got drawn into an unusual situation.

It was like this. A year or two earlier, Louis Malle, an internationally celebrated French film-maker, had approached the government in Delhi for permission to make a documentary film on Calcutta. After the usual formalities, permission was gladly granted to the famous film-maker. When the film was made and shown to officials of the government, they found it not presentable and withheld permission to screen it. It was said that Malle had presented the city in very poor light. Embassies and missions abroad were told to prevent the film from being screened. Around this time, I was approached by the Austrian government TV channel. They were going to screen *Calcutta* as part of their popular programme called 'Contra', in which two conflicting and contrary views were presented on a chosen subject. They wanted a film to be given to them for screening that would show the other side of what Louis Malle had shown in his film, so that viewers could get the chance to see both sides.

I wrote to S. K. Singh, who was heading the External Publicity Division in the MEA in Delhi (he later became Foreign Secretary and eventually the Governor of Rajasthan). My proposal to him was that we should provide a film made by a Swedish film-maker, Arne Sucksdorff, a few years earlier, called *The Flute and the Arrow* (1957). The film was made on the life of tribal people in Bastar (which is now in Chhattisgarh and was then in Madhya Pradesh). It was a sensitively made film which captured the natural environment in which people lived in harmony with nature, and had been greatly appreciated by then Prime Minister, Jawaharlal Nehru. A copy of the film, which had been presented to Nehru, would be available in the Nehru Memorial Museum and Library at Teen Murti Bhavan. Mr Singh replied that there was no question of providing a film of our choice for the 'Contra' programme. In fact, he was of the opinion that we should not allow the screening of Louis Malle's

Calcutta in the programme at all. He had not seen *The Flute and the Arrow*, nor was he interested in seeing it.

The TV channel was adamant about screening *Calcutta*. I was unable to persuade them not to do so. They insisted that we provide them with a film of our choice. I could not persuade the Foreign Ministry in Delhi to do that either. My failure on both fronts and my suggestion that a film on Adivasi life be screened in the 'Contra' programme came in for much criticism in the Ministry. What puzzled me was that Ambassador Trivedi, who was a much admired and very senior official, much senior to S. K. Singh, did not offer me his advice, nor did he prevent me from taking a different course on the issue. He maintained complete silence throughout.

I watched *Calcutta*, as did a very large audience which used to wait for the 'Contra' programme. The film was a powerful depiction of a city burdened by poverty and inequality, by filth and the remains of a colonial legacy. The camera showed mountains of garbage on the streets and wide avenues where children and pigs together searched for something they could eat, even if it was mango seeds already sucked clean. The film captured the crowds at heavily decorated Durga Puja pandals. It showed the destitute state of daily wage earners, who lived and cooked under the sky on footpaths next to towering buildings which they constructed. Unlike normal documentary films which have background music, Malle's camera captured the actual sounds and noises of the overflowing city. I was familiar with Calcutta. It is my *sasural* (in-laws' home). My husband was born and brought up in North Calcutta. His family still lives there, close to Shyambazar, one of the oldest and most traditional parts of the city. Malle's *Calcutta* struck me as an honest and powerful depiction of the city built by the British and further perpetuated in the same way, drawing people from the hinterland who made a living on the city's footpaths.

What puzzled me then was the reluctance of our government to show and even see the other India, the Adivasi way of life, a hesitation that continues even today. It is a part of the country that colonial Britain could not penetrate, despite its many attempts. These are forests where the original or Adivasi people live. The size of the area is vast and much greater than the mega-cities of Mumbai, Delhi, Kolkata, Chennai, and Bengaluru combined. It spreads over Madhya Pradesh, Odisha, Andhra Pradesh, Telangana, Chhattisgarh, and parts of Maharashtra. The struggle of the Adivasi communities to retain their own ways of life and resist being drawn into Louis Malle's *Calcutta* footpaths and mountains of garbage is seen as 'anti-development'. Their struggle is now labelled as 'internal terrorism'.

What has made things worse is the more recent discovery of vast natural resources under the forests, which have been home to the Adivasis for as long as one knows. What I wanted to know then was why the government was in denial; why it refused to admit the existence of this part of India and its people who live close to and in harmony with nature. Although census data may not admit it, Adivasi communities are not Hindu. They do not have caste divisions. Perhaps that is also why their hamlets and villages are clean. The cleanliness of Adivasi areas is in stark contrast to the villages, towns, and cities of India. Santhal Adivasi[1] villages in Bengal are in fact aesthetically very appealing. Not only do the Adivasis not have caste divisions, but the gender divide is also much less sharp among them.

Perhaps the cleanliness of Adivasi life could be attributed to the fact that there are no 'higher' castes among them who have the privilege of creating filth which the 'lower' castes alone are obliged to clean up. The drive towards cleanliness and a 'Swachh Bharat' today seems to me unlikely to succeed till the caste distinction between the 'privileged' creators of filth and the 'lower-caste' cleaners is removed. Till the time that maintaining cleanliness becomes everyone's equal responsibility, a clean India is not likely to emerge.

In Vienna, Amit, an economist who was then working with UNIDO (United Nations Industrial Development Organization), and I lived on Stephansplatz, on the third floor of a building bang opposite the Stephansdom (church), around which the city of Vienna had evolved over centuries. On Sundays and Wednesdays, we could hear the sound of music from the church by just opening our windows. When I was asked where I lived, my reply often amazed people. Living on Stephansplatz in Vienna is like living opposite the Taj Mahal in India.

I often parked my little Volkswagen car, a Beetle, in the area around the Hofburg Palace. In those days, most international conferences were held in the large halls of the Palace. The President of Austria resides in a part of the same Palace. Since a lot of my time was spent in conferences, especially of the International Atomic Energy Agency (IAEA) where India was under considerable pressure to sign the Treaty on the Non-Proliferation of Nuclear Weapons (NPT), I was well-acquainted with the area. It was also a short walking distance from our home. In 1972, Amit and I travelled around Europe, and before leaving, I parked the car in a corner of the area around the Hofburg Palace. When we returned three weeks later, I was warned by the Ambassador's social secretary that the police had not taken well to my choice of parking place. The next morning when I approached the car, a police officer looked like she was waiting for me. I took fright because I had heard that female police officers were supposedly stricter, and unrelenting to persuasion.

'So, you could not find a more suitable place to park your car for three weeks?' she taunted.

I had no suitable answer.

'Do diplomats in your country park their cars in your presidential palace?' Her tone was loaded with sarcasm.

'No. They are not allowed to do so, definitely not,' I replied.

'So?' she asked.

'Well, there is no sign here saying that parking is not allowed,' I said, looking around in support of my claim. 'We have signs saying that parking is not allowed,' I added humbly. What I did not say was that cars are not allowed within half-a-kilometre of the Rashtrapati Bhavan without proof of an appointment. 'Please show me a "No Parking" sign here,' I requested her.

The fact is that even today, there is no such sign near the Hofburg Palace. One can park one's car there, and many people do so.

Around that time, a public outcry resembling a storm broke out in the otherwise orderly city of Vienna. It started with a new rule which banned dogs from playing on the green grass of the city's many beautifully maintained parks. The Viennese were great dog lovers. They raised the objection: If children were allowed to play on the grass, why not their loyal dogs? The outrage of the dog lovers and their strong protests forced the city administration to withdraw the ban.

What I found amazing was that the people of Vienna had actually protested, and forcefully so, to protect the rights of their pets. Four decades earlier, this had not happened when Jews, who constituted 25 per cent of the population of the city, were persecuted, humiliated, and looted. Hitler did not conquer Austria; Austrians welcomed him with open arms. On a night in November 1938, which came to be known as '*Kristallnacht*' (The Night of Broken Glass), Jews were dragged out, their shops and homes were broken, and every type of humiliation was meted out to them by the SA (*Sturmabteilung*, literally 'Storm Detachment' in German) paramilitary forces and German civilians. This November pogrom, carried out throughout Nazi Germany, Austria, and Sudetenland, came to be known as the 'Night of Broken Glass' or 'Crystal Night' because of the shards of broken glass that littered the streets from the shattered windows of Jewish-owned stores, buildings, and synagogues. Later, the arrested Jews were forcibly moved to be killed in gas chambers in concentration camps.[2] The Austrians, a people who loved music, literature, art, and science, showed very little humanism then. They did not protest. It baffled me.

On the subject of protest, I am reminded of my own one-woman failure. It was like this. Amit and I were married under the Special Marriage Act in the house of our Ambassador in Vienna.

The Ambassador's residence is legally regarded as 'India'. My parents were witnesses and the only guest present was Mira Behn, who was once a close associate of Mahatma Gandhi and lived in Vienna. Ambassador Trivedi wanted us to be photographed and chose Frau Simoniz, a very well-known photographer, for the purpose. Frau Simoniz went about her task with so much care and patience that we were exhausted at the end of it all. The photographs turned out to be quite professional.

Then suddenly, one morning while crossing the road in front of Hotel Bristol, opposite the Opera House, right in the heart of the city, I saw something unbelievable. Hanging at the tram stop was a large photograph of my husband and I. It was one of those taken by Frau Simoniz. Instead of walking to the Embassy, I went straight to her studio and told her that she had no business displaying our photograph by hanging it in the centre of town. 'You look so nice!' she said. 'I don't want to be part of your advertisement campaign!' I objected, and insisted that she remove the photograph. I even made a written protest, but to no avail. She ignored my raving and my protests and kept us hanging in the centre of town for several weeks.

Notes

1. Santhals are native mainly to the states of Jharkhand, Assam, Tripura, Odisha, Bihar, Chhattisgarh, and West Bengal.

2. Historians have come to regard the *'Kristallnacht'* as a prelude to the 'Final Solution' and genocide of six million Jews across Nazi Germany and German-occupied Europe during the Holocaust.

2

New Delhi, 1973

From Vienna, I was posted back to Delhi where I was given the charge as Undersecretary in the West Europe Division in the Ministry of External Affairs (MEA).

In the summer of 1973, early one morning I was summoned to the Ministry by Mr Ahuja, one of the three senior-most officials in the Ministry. A car came to take me to his office at 7 AM. The size of the long foreign-made limousine was daunting. This was the era of Ambassador and Fiat cars. When I met Mr Ahuja in his office, he told me that I had been summoned to take up an 'important responsibility'. I was to look after a visiting dignitary, Princess Ashraf Pahlavi of Iran, who was arriving within a few hours. She was the twin sister of His Imperial Highness, the Shah of Iran. I asked him why I was being given this responsibility when I was not dealing with Iran. 'The Prime Minister has chosen you for the task,' he told me, which was to silence me, and it did.

Mr Ahuja continued, 'The last time when the Princess came at our invitation, she left in a huff within a few hours. This should not happen again. You understand?' I nodded. 'We want her to go back very happy with her stay as our guest,' he said.

Mr Ahuja had been Ambassador in Tehran and knew the country well. He continued, saying, 'The Princess is a difficult person. She is arrogant, ill-mannered and ill-tempered, and easily provoked to anger. Your task is not easy. She will be staying in Rashtrapati Bhavan. The four ministers of the Government of Iran who are accompanying her will also be staying there. On our part, our Minister of Education, Professor Nurul Hassan, will be the minster in waiting. You are also being given a room in Rashtrapati Bhavan and a car along with every facility. She is arriving in an hour from now in her own private aircraft from Tehran.' He looked at his watch. 'We should move to the airport now,' he said.

There was nothing for me to do but to take his instructions seriously. He handed me a copy of the minute-by-minute programme of Her Imperial Highness, which included meetings with the Prime Minister.

At the airport, we were told that the arrival time of the VIP plane was uncertain. In true imperial style, we were all kept waiting. Professor Hassan had to answer questions in Parliament, so he was forced to leave. Mr Ahuja looked unhappy. However, it was decided that the education minister would arrive at Rashtrapati Bhavan directly from Parliament House to welcome the Princess, as soon as his responsibilities in Parliament were over.

At Rashtrapati Bhavan, Mohini Giri, the daughter of the President, was waiting with flowers to welcome the Princess who, without looking at her, walked straight to her suite. Professor Hassan arrived within a few minutes. He was a very gentle and sophisticated person who was well-known for his research work in history. None of the four ministers from Iran engaged him in conversation while he was kept waiting. After close to forty-five minutes of his waiting, I asked the Iranian Minister of Education if he should not inform Her Imperial Highness that our minister had been waiting for almost an hour. In reply, he indicated her door, saying, 'You should do that yourself'. I knocked at her door and entered, and was taken aback. The Princess had come out after a bath and was holding a cup of tea. She was not wearing anything. One of the ministers was holding her robe and another was holding her lipstick. With some courage, I approached her with a smile and told her that our minister was waiting to greet and welcome her.

When she finally emerged, she threw one glance at Professor Nurul Hassan and then did not look at him again while he explained the circumstances which had not allowed him to wait for Her Imperial Highness at the airport. His apology fell on deaf ears. The manner in which she treated him made me wonder if she would not once again cut short her visit to Delhi like the last time. She did not once smile or acknowledge Professor Hassan, even when he got up and left.

Ms Giri tried to make conversation with the Princess. She said that the art of miniature paintings had come from Iran to India during the Mughal period and that over centuries, some individual schools of miniature painting had evolved in India. A good private collection of this art was available in Calcutta with the Goenka family. If the Princess was interested, we could get that collection transported and exhibited in Rashtrapati Bhavan. Her Imperial Highness did not respond, not even with a nod. There was an awkwardness deliberately imposed by her, it seemed to me.

When lunch was ready to be served, I informed the Iranian education minister and he gave me the same reply, 'Please tell her yourself and stay with her for lunch'. I soon found that I was alone in looking after our imperial guest, whose visit was of paramount importance because India was hopeful of exporting Kudremukh iron-ore[1] to Iran.

As I discovered, the Princess was bitter partly because she was the twin sister of the Shah of Iran. She was born a few hours before him but because she was a female, the crown had been denied to her. She had little interest in food. She liked to have tea every few hours and something to munch with it. The cooks were told to put their best snacks before her with her tea.

The next day, Ms Giri sent me a message to say that the Goenka collection of miniature paintings had arrived from Calcutta and a professional team had set up an exhibition of it in Rashtrapati Bhavan for the Princess. 'Should we go to see the exhibition?' I asked Her Imperial Highness.

'You can see it. I am not interested,' she replied. 'What would you like to see?' I asked her. 'Bombay films are good, aren't they?' she said. 'Is there any particular film that you would like to see?' I asked her. *Pakeezah*, was her reply. Then she asked me, 'Have you seen it?' 'I have heard of it, but I haven't seen it,' I told her. 'Then you can also see it,' she suggested.

'When would you like to see it?' I asked her. 'This evening,' she replied. 'But this evening you are dining with the Prime Minister,' I reminded her. 'We will see it after the dinner,' she said.

I immediately ordered that *Pakeezah*, starring Meena Kumari, should be procured from Mumbai for screening at the private auditorium of Rashtrapati Bhavan late that evening.

In the afternoon, when the royal guest was resting and I was deep into Joseph Conrad's novel *The Secret Agent* (1907), there was a knock at my door. On opening it, I was confronted with many of the staff of the President's estate, who were looking very serious. 'What is the matter?' I asked. 'Madam, we have been working here for years, but have never been asked to do this sort of work…it is not for us,' the oldest among them said. 'What sort of work are you being asked to do which is objectionable?' I wanted to know. 'We go with trays of tea and snacks for the guest…and she is not dressed… she is wearing nothing.'

I remembered my own surprise when I had entered her room on the first day. Now this was a real challenge. 'Our guest speaks a different language; she comes from a different tradition. We cannot tell our guests to speak in our language or behave in the way we behave. We have no choice but to accept them as they are. Our responsibility is to look after them well. On that, there can be no compromise. No compromise. If you are offended by her not being dressed as you would like, please go with your trays and do not look at her,' I told them. The delegation left quietly but unhappily.

At eight in the evening, I accompanied Her Imperial Highness to Mrs Gandhi's house, where the Prime Minister was waiting on the porch to receive her guest. This was unprecedented. When I returned to pick up our imperial guest, both she and the Prime Minister looked happy. Indira Gandhi asked me if I was being well looked after. This was typical of her.

'You will be showing us *Pakeezah* now?' the Princess wanted to be reassured when we were in the car on our way back. I nodded.

Her Imperial Highness, along with her ministers and other members of her delegation, trooped into the auditorium holding bottles of whiskey. Along with the flowing spirits, they enjoyed the film. Meena Kumari's charm worked its way into their hearts. The evening ended splendidly.

At the request of our guests, the large jewellery shop of Bhimsen Jhaweri in Janpath was opened only for the Iranian guests the next day. Her Imperial Highness also saw an exhibition of Indian handicrafts. She was generally unimpressed. Iran had so much better and more to offer, she told me. Her visit ended without what Mr Ahuja had called a tantrum.

Five years later in 1978, the Shah of Iran was to come for a State visit to India. By then, things had changed somewhat. The prices of oil had made Iran and its neighbouring Arab States very rich. India wanted better relations with them. Morarji Desai was Prime Minister in Delhi. In Iran, rumblings of political protest against the Shah's regime were gaining momentum. Protests were also carried out by Iranian students studying in various Indian universities. The Iranian government wanted these Iranian 'anti-national' student protesters to be deported back to Iran, and requested the Government of India to do so. The higher-ranking Indian officials were inclined to oblige the Iranian authorities in the interest of improving relations with oil-rich Iran. A director in the External Affairs Ministry had the courage to write to the Prime Minister, stating that deporting the Iranian students would mean sending them to their deaths. Anti-national elements in Iran generally met that fate. The note written by Akbar Khalili changed the government's stand, and the lives of the student protesters were saved, even at the cost of annoying the Iranian authorities. Khalili had a grain of humanism and the courage to speak his mind. This is something which appears to have disappeared from the ranks of government officials. Had there been an Akbar Khalili, or someone like him, the sword hanging over the heads of students like Rohith Vemula could have been lifted in time to save him from taking his life, and the inhuman treatment of alleged 'anti-national' students in many universities in the country could have been avoided as well.

Within a year of the very successful visit of the Shah of Iran to India, he was overthrown in the culmination of the Iranian Revolution of 1979. Those who had been anti-national forces then became national heroes. History, it would appear, does not allow such labels to stick for too long.

On the West Europe desk, which I was handling, I often received information from the Home Ministry about citizens of European countries who had been arrested for not having valid visas or for having overstayed without permission. I used to pass this information on to the embassies in Delhi of the respective countries of these arrested people. Many of them were deported back to their countries. One such case was that of a young French woman who had overstayed beyond her visa. I sent the information of her arrest to the French Embassy. The response came, to my surprise, from the French Ambassador himself. He wanted to meet my boss, the Head of the West Europe Division, immediately to discuss this case. The French behaviour is normally more hierarchical than even Indian behaviour. French Ambassadors did not speak to junior officers in the Ministry. The Ambassador, whom I received on arrival and accompanied to the office of my boss, was very excited. He informed us (I was present to take down the minutes of the meeting) that the young woman whose arrest I had informed them about was the daughter of a very dear friend of his. She was the only child of one of the richest men in his country.

As it happened, she was not in good shape. When I met her, she looked like she had not eaten in days and was in a dishevelled state of appearance. She did not speak at all. The rules did not permit an arrested foreigner to be handed over to the Embassy. Since the French Ambassador insisted that he wanted her to be handed over to him so that she could be given a chance to have a good meal and be properly dressed before he sent her to her father, who was his close friend, it required the concurrence of our External Affairs Minister and Home Minister. This procedure took time and the French Ambassador lived through a stressful period of waiting till the arrested young woman accompanied him one afternoon. She was to take the flight to Paris the next morning.

To my utter amazement, the next morning I found His Excellency, the French Ambassador, waiting outside my office. He was in tears. 'She ran away at night,' he said to me. He pleaded with me to get the Delhi police to find her. He did not know how to face her father, and what to say to him.

The Home Ministry had many such cases on its hands. This was the time of the flower children. It was an era when India attracted a lot of young men and women in search of freedom and a carefree, career-free life. Many of them landed in police custody.

A few weeks after this incident, Amit and I went for a holiday to the hill town of Manali. We stayed in a forest bungalow which was a short distance away from the town. One morning, as we were returning from the market as usual with groceries and a day-old newspaper, I saw Amit, who was about ten steps ahead of me (because I was busy looking at the newspaper headlines), take out his wallet to give something to a beggar. As I came nearer, the beggar saw me. As soon as our eyes met, she took fright and ran as fast as she could, as though I was the police on the lookout for her, to catch and send her back to her father in Paris. Manali was then, and perhaps still is, a sought-after place for drug addicts.

Notes

1. Kudremukh iron-ore is found in the Chikmagalur district of Karnataka. The Kudremukh mine was one of the largest iron-ore mines in the world and was closed in 2006.

3

Vietnam, 1975

In January 1975, I received an order posting me as First Secretary to the Embassy in Hanoi, North Vietnam. My father was distraught upon hearing this news. 'It is raining bombs there, why do you want to be posted to Vietnam?' he said.

Vietnam had been the focus of world attention. That tiny underdeveloped ('developing', in today's parlance) country had been fighting, in succession, first Japan, then France, and was now at war with America, the world's number one superpower. Vietnam was fighting to unite the divided North with the South. America, as usual, was fighting for freedom and democracy, as it continued to do in many parts of the world, recently in West Asia. In universities and information media within America, critical voices had become louder and fiercer against America's war in Vietnam. The carpet bombings and chemical warfare in Central and South Vietnam were being deplored. Prime Minister Indira Gandhi called for an end to the bombing of Vietnam. This was an act of courage because during this time, India was critically dependent on shipments of wheat under American Public Law 480. In Asia, or for that matter all over the world, there was no non-communist country which dared to raise its voice.

My departure to Hanoi was postponed because Prabhakar Menon, whom I was to replace, could not leave Hanoi before the new ambassador had taken over. In the meantime, on 30 April, American forces withdrew from Saigon, leaving behind them a legacy of devastation and a large cache of arms and ammunition after their defeat at the hands of a small country which had no air or naval power. On the evening of 30 April 1975, the campus of Jawaharlal Nehru University (JNU) reverberated with slogans of 'Long live, Vietnam!' Vietnamese students sang patriotic songs in a charged atmosphere at an open-air gathering. We used to live on the campus because Amit was a professor there.

I travelled to Hanoi by air up to Hong Kong, and then proceeded by train to Canton. The last leg of the journey, from Nanning to Hanoi, was concluded by a short flight on a Chinese aircraft. The Haiphong harbour was yet to be cleared of mines, so my heavy baggage travelled from Delhi to Hanoi via Moscow. This might appear funny today, but the fact that politics takes over geography is something I have experienced very closely.

There were at the time very few diplomatic missions in Hanoi. And with few exceptions like the Indian and French Embassies, the rest were accommodated in a hotel built in the early twentieth century during French rule. Because India had been Chairman of the Peace Commission for Indo-China, we were allotted three villas for the Embassy and also had the best interpreter, who was intelligent as well as a fine person. The hotel accommodation of other diplomatic missions was limited. The Ambassadors of Australia and Japan were among them, and had to convert their bedrooms into offices during the day. They had attached bathrooms, but common toilet facilities. The bathrooms also doubled as kitchens to cater to parties, which were regularly held in the most undiplomatic traditions. I must admit that these were among the most enjoyable parties because they were improvised in imaginative ways, and were not the usual representational functions which diplomats around the world are obliged to suffer. Since the Indian Embassy had villas, the backyard of one of them (where I lived) was converted into a proper badminton court. Almost all diplomats in Hanoi learnt to play badminton; those who did not, came on their bicycles to watch and chat. Hanoi provided little by way of entertainment.

Before leaving for Hanoi, I was advised to carry all my requirements, from toothpaste, washing powder and soap, to milk powder, with me. Nothing more than the food items needed for daily consumption were available in the markets. On my arrival, I used some of my saris to make curtains for the windows. A Vietnamese citizen was provided with five metres of cloth every year, along with food, soap, and everything else s/he needed. Everyone had a bicycle, just as everyone had a roof. I had also acquired a bicycle. Diplomatic missions had a car each, but almost every diplomat rode a bicycle.

I was provided a cook and a maid to care for my house and kitchen. Ain Thai was a good cook. I taught him to cook some Indian dishes, and showed him how to make yoghurt with the milk powder I had brought along with me from Hong Kong. He had a quick grasp over things and made good yoghurt for about ten days. Then he politely asked me, 'Are you sick?' I was puzzled. Pointing at the small bowl of yoghurt, he said, 'Then why do you eat this?' It struck me suddenly that my eating yoghurt made from animal milk must have nauseated him. In China and Vietnam, milk is regarded as essential only for new-born babies. Otherwise, it is treated as an animal discharge, like urine, sweat, etc. It was unfair of me to have made him handle milk powder. I told him not to make yoghurt for me and that I would make it myself. Soya milk and cheese were easily available, and I learnt to enjoy them also.

I wondered how my mother, who was a vegetarian, would view this. Like most, if not all Indians, she considered milk and its products the best for health and the ideal food for the gods. To think that somewhere in the world God's food was nauseating would have shocked her. She would have been equally shocked to see that except for cats, almost all other animals were eaten with relish. The adage 'One man's meat is another man's poison' is literally true.

The second lesson I learnt was something like this. The Canadian Ambassador in China had come for a visit to Hanoi just around the time that I went there. He asked me if in India, too, people did not apologise. In China, there was no equivalent to 'I am sorry'. Was this a tradition all over Asia? I told him that it was not so in India, and I began noticing how the people in Vietnam said sorry.

The matter was handled quite differently there. Instead of waiting for someone to apologise, the person is offered an opportunity to save face. If I am late in arriving, I will immediately be handed an excuse: the road is bad, or a family member is ill, etc. If it is a deeper matter, then the offender gives an explanation called 'self-criticism'. I found the offer to save face quite comfortable and more generous than waiting for 'I am sorry'.

Initially, while I was in Hanoi, Amit was in Bangkok planning to fly to Hanoi via Vientiane (Laos). I was suddenly told by a Vietnamese friend that the situation in Laos was such that flights between Vientiane and Bangkok would come to a halt after two days. I requested David Wilson, the Australian Ambassador who was flying to Bangkok via Hong Kong that day, to pass this information on to Amit. David Wilson took my concerns seriously. He met Amit and put him on the last flight leaving Bangkok for Vientiane. I was to meet Amit in Vientiane, but that became impossible. Just then, the communist revolution arrived in Laos. Amit found himself in a city where everything had come to a sudden standstill. Markets were shut down and, worse, banks were closed for four days. He was stuck in a totally unknown place in the midst of a change of system. He later wrote an account in Bangla about the unnerving, and sometimes comical, experience of his stay in Vientiane during that period.

What created problems for us was the fact that Vietnam was not connected by telephone or even telegraphic links with most parts of the world. It was not a member of the International Postal System. Today, this might sound like a joke, but the reality of the time was such that my letters to Amit left every fortnight by diplomatic bag via a courier, who went to Hong Kong. From there, they went by Air India to Delhi. The letters were posted in Delhi for Bangkok. It took more than a month for my letters to reach, and it took almost two months for his to reach me by the same reverse route. In today's world of instant communication, it sounds almost prehistoric. It certainly was not easy.

Finally, Amit arrived in Hanoi. By this time winter had also arrived, but we had no warm clothes because our heavy baggage was still stuck in Moscow. I turned to Mr Glasnost, my counterpart in the Soviet Embassy, for his help. A few days later, I saw him coming to my office, taking two steps at a time in a state of excitement. 'Your baggage has come!' he said, and drove me to the tiny rickety airport where a Russian cargo plane was opening its underbelly, from which came gushing out potatoes. Among them, I spotted a few boxes of my books and warm clothes tumbling out.

At the time of my posting to Hanoi, and because I had volunteered for this hard posting, *The Times of India* had carried a report on it. If I remember right, it had even called me 'courageous'. This might have been the reason why I was given a somewhat favourable, if not special, treatment by the Vietnamese government. For instance, I got my driving licence at the first test, whereas the British Ambassador had taken the test several times but failed to make it. The application of my boss, the Indian Ambassador, appeared to have been lost because he was not called for the test at all. When I asked a friend why the British Ambassador could not qualify when he had several more years of driving experience than I and was a pilot as well, the answer was that the British did not blink when Vietnam was being destroyed.

One evening, I was invited to dinner by the Information Ministry. After a banquet-like meal and several toasts raised to India–Vietnam friendship, a personal request was made to me. Vietnam was going to enter, for the first time, a film at an international film festival. They needed help in dubbing the film into English. Could I help them? I told them that I had no experience in this field. Besides, English was not my mother tongue. I suggested that the British Ambassador's wife might be much better suited for this. This suggestion was met with the polite reply that my Vietnamese friends preferred my English.

I remember that when I told my Ambassador about this request, he asked me, 'How will they return your favour?' This had not occurred to me. I accepted the request.

Every afternoon, a car came to fetch me and drove to a point at one of the largest and quietest lakes of Hanoi, from where a boat took us to a small island on the lake. A sound studio had been made at this very tranquil place with East German help. The walls and roof were stuffed with cloth to make it soundproof. There, I embarked on my first and last venture in dubbing. I liked the film (the name of which I cannot recall), which was on the unpredictable nature of life in war-time. Nothing was how it should have been. Emotional stress and strain were reflected in the stormy winds which blew everything away. There was a note of understatement running through the story, which was moving. After an hour and a half of work, we would normally take a break outside the studio where delicious cut fruit was offered as refreshment. I wondered why our cook Ain Thai could not buy such papayas and pineapples. When I asked him, his answer was that he could have had access to the best quality of everything if he were a member of the government, but alas, he was only a nobody.

One afternoon, just as the dubbing was proceeding with concentration, a sudden loud sound brought everything to a halt. It turned out that the sound had been made by a very large lizard. I have never before, nor since, seen such a large and dominating animal of this kind. We had probably disturbed it during its afternoon siesta. I was terrified. The others just laughed it off. Work was resumed.

At my request, Amit and I had been provided with a teacher from whom we were learning Vietnamese. He was a good teacher, but we were not half as good as students and the language is very tough, so progress was slow.

One of my most memorable experiences in Hanoi was the celebration of victory in the Vietnam War in September 1975. The entire population of the town and the villages surrounding it came to the central lake of Hanoi on their bicycles and watched a magnificent display of fireworks. Chinese fireworks are renowned. They were all the more imposing because the brilliant flares of colours leaping up to touch the evening sky were reflected in the still clear waters of the lake below. It was a befitting celebration to mark the end of a long and devastating war. There were no speeches, no patriotic songs. It was just a bewitching spectacle, one not easy to forget. At the end of it, people gradually moved away and rode back home on their bicycles. There were no police in uniform. There was no one to supervise the people who had assembled and no one to 'control' an 'unruly' crowd in a hurry. No one was in a hurry.

I had noticed this at the railway station as well. No one was in a hurry. People were confident that they would get their turn to carry their bicycles into the empty train carriages. It struck me that a nation which had fought an unequal war was less violent than Indians committed to 'nonviolence'. Perhaps we needed a lesson in nonviolence more than other societies.

I requested the Vietnamese Foreign Office to be allowed to visit Saigon and other areas in South Vietnam, which had been especially targeted for carpet-bombing and chemical weapons. North and South Vietnam were still to be united. The South was under the Provisional Revolutionary Government, whose chief was Madame Binh. Saigon was yet to be named Ho Chi Minh City. No diplomat in Hanoi had made this journey, not even Russian and Chinese diplomats. Central Vietnam was cut off because most of its towns were uninhabited ruins. Amit and I had visited Vinh in Central Vietnam, which had only one small brick house left standing, surrounded by ruins. There was no connectivity between the North and the South except through small government airplanes since Central Vietnam had been completely ravaged by bombing. My request to visit Saigon and Cu Chi was accepted and arrangements were made to take me there.

I travelled in a small Soviet-made aircraft along with eight other *dong chi* (comrades). One of them was a woman who spent the entire journey knitting. She seemed to me to be a nurse. The seats were in the shape of overturned buckets. The scene at the airport in Saigon took me by surprise. There were unending lines of American air force fighter planes that had been left behind by the defeated army. I recalled a conversation between the Foreign Minister of Vietnam, Nguyen Co Thaic, and the Indian Ambassador a few evenings ago. Our Ambassador, Chinmay Gharekhan, had said that the Southeast Asian neighbours of Vietnam were apprehensive that the latter might use the sophisticated weaponry left behind by the Americans to export revolution to their countries. The Foreign Minister had laughingly replied that if technologically superior weaponry could win wars, then America would not have lost to Vietnam. He assured Ambassador Gharekhan that Vietnam's neighbours had no reason to be apprehensive.

I was put up in a hotel close to river Saigon, the walls of which still had holes made by gunshots. Buildings still looked devastated, but life in the city appeared to be moving normally. Unlike in Hanoi, where markets were limited to selling only food items, here they were selling every conceivable item. Young women beautifully dressed in their traditional *áo dài* (a long split tunic dress worn over trousers) were on bicycles and the city restaurants were doing good business. Saigon had been called the Paris of the East. It was still very attractive, even chic. In this environment, the very young Viet Cong soldiers known as *Bodoi*, from the villages, were misfits. They looked lost. Outside a large department store, one of them asked me if he could go in. I assured him that it was his city and he should not hesitate. Later, I heard many jokes about the innocence of the *Bodois*, which supposedly bordered on stupidity; such was the way they were viewed in Saigon.

Arrangements had been made for me to leave for Cu Chi in a jeep along with a *dong chi* very early in the morning. As we drove out of the city at dawn, the landscape gradually began transforming into larger and larger bomb craters on all sides, till finally, as far as the eye could see, there was no sign of life. Not even a blade of grass. It could have been a landscape on the moon.

Cu Chi was the forested area, once thickly covered with rubber trees and tall bamboos, under which the Viet Cong had dug deep tunnels and created a fighting base complete with hospitals, kitchens, and living quarters for the soldiers. This is why it was made the target of the worst bombings. Anything that was left intact was burnt with Agent Orange, a deadly chemical.

By afternoon, we had reached a small hamlet of bamboo mud huts. Except for a young pregnant woman, all the inhabitants had gone out to level the ground, I was told. Since I had stepped out of a government vehicle, the young woman asked me if I was a Russian. I told her that I was not a '*Lin So*' (Russian) but an '*An Do*' (Indian).

She had no idea what an *'An Do'* or Indian was, just as she had no idea what a Russian looked like.

A little further, a team was working to level the ground. They had only shovels and bamboo baskets to fill a large bomb crater with mud. I wondered how long it would take to fill those innumerable and unending holes. It seemed to me to be an impossible task. Finally, we arrived at the administrative centre. I was greeted by the *dong chi* in charge of the centre which, like the huts we had seen, was also made of bamboo and mud. I was offered a cup of hot water which did not have the usual green tea leaves. 'Things are bleak now, but on your next visit I will offer you a cup of fragrant tea,' he said. He was reassuring and answered all my questions, although I was not convinced when he said that they had a bulldozer. I did not see one and could hardly believe that even if there was one, it would have the fuel it needed to run in this desolate place.

That visit to Cu Chi was disturbing. It seemed to me that winning a war against a powerful adversary is a big achievement, but reconstructing on the destruction left behind is an equally challenging task. When I was leaving, my host said to me very sincerely, 'When you come next, we will share with you a meal of rice grown here.'

In Saigon, there was a small population of people of Indian origin. The French administration had shipped Tamil labour from Pondicherry (now renamed Puducherry) to work in Vietnam, just like the British had taken shiploads of Biharis to far-off places like Trinidad. The Tamil labourers had married Vietnamese women. Their children had no connection with India. They spoke Vietnamese, and some of them spoke French or English, but no one spoke any Indian language. Among them, there were some who had become businessmen and traders. I met some of them who had been serving long jail terms in prison on charges of tax evasion. Soon after the sudden withdrawal of American forces on 30 April 1975, when the prison gates were opened, these convicts, among others, also got their freedom. They were, of course, fearful of the imminent move towards socialism and saw no future for themselves in Vietnam. They appealed for help to the Indian government to leave Vietnam. This was the time when many Vietnamese in the South were fleeing from communism in rickety boats on the high seas. There were daily reports of these boats sinking, or their passengers being saved by commercial ships.

Some of the Indian businessmen were very well-to-do. But they were determined not to buy their way on commercial airlines to leave Vietnam. I informed them that Air France was still running its flights from Saigon to Paris for a few more days, and that it would be wise to avail of this opportunity before it ceased. They were adamant that the Government of India should provide them with free air transport to leave Saigon. Finally, an Air India plane transported them free of cost to Madras, from where they made their way to France or America. Many of their children visit a completely transformed Vietnam for vacations these days.

In September 2015, Amit and I also travelled to Vietnam after forty years. We had been hearing from friends who had been there that things had changed, yet I was taken aback by what I saw. Those tiny bamboo huts with thatched roofs had disappeared. Their place was taken by colourful brick houses, two or three stories high. These thin and tall red, blue, green, and yellow structures were strange and yet attractive. Those wide avenues around the many lakes of Hanoi, which had exclusively bicycle traffic then, were now crowded with buzzing motorcycles. The few bicycles one saw were being pedalled by children. What had remained unchanged was the sight of women tending their farms on the outskirts of the city, wearing the same large cone-shaped palm-leaf hats which protect them from sun and rain.

Like Bangalore, Hanoi is a city of many large and small lakes. But unlike Bangalore, Hanoi's lakes are clean and clear. In the race towards development, they have not been used for sewage disposal like the lakes and rivers of India. The markets of downtown Hanoi are no less crowded and bustling with activity than our markets. But they are clean, again unlike our markets. We stayed at a small hotel in what used to be and is still called the 'Old Quarter'. Forty years ago, the Old Quarter was a run-down part of the town with rickety wooden huts. Only the courageous among the small diplomatic community then dared to go there.

The Old Quarter today has a bustling market for almost everything one might like to buy. It also has the best eateries in town, which come alive as the evening progresses. Wooden benches and tables take over the narrow streets, where young couples enjoy local beer and sea food. One wonders if Delhi's Chandni Chowk will ever turn into a lively meeting place like this. Not in our lifetime.

We left Hanoi for Hue on our way to Ho Chi Minh City. Hue, situated halfway between the North and the South of the country, used to be the capital once, from where the king used to rule. The town was totally destroyed during American bombing. Only those inhabitants who could run away in time were saved. In short, the entire city of Hue has been reconstructed after the war. Some ruins of the old capital have been restored. So has an old monastery, which is situated at a height overlooking a bend in the river Perfume. It is a most beautiful sight where monks, including women monks, reside. It has a history of playing a leading role in the county's struggle for reunification.

In the evenings, the river, which is the pride of the city, comes alive when large, illuminated boats offer music concerts along with a ride. We enjoyed this outing and found ourselves the only foreign tourists among the audience, who were nostalgic for Vietnamese songs as they played in a boat made to invite the evening breeze.

The sea around Hue is a hub of the fishing industry. Basa fish has a growing export market, including India and America. The population of Vietnam, which was forty-five million forty years ago, has doubled to ninety million now. The per capita income has far overtaken that of India. The country has full literacy and a healthcare system which covers all its villages, towns, and cities.

Saigon, which is now Ho Chi Minh City, has many attractions. The one which is a must for any visitor is the War Remnants Museum. Museums can be interesting, but this one is moving. It has a collection of articles and photographs by journalists from France, England, Germany, Italy, and America, who had documented the war in Vietnam from dangerously close quarters. Some of them lost their lives in the process, but have left behind live accounts. The Viet Cong had no cameras, nor the time for journalism. Outside the museum, one can see the fighter jets which had rained bombs during the war. The then American General, Westmoreland, had boasted that Vietnam would be bombed back to the Stone Age. Forty years ago, I had personally seen the Stone Age in Cu Chi.

I was eager to revisit Cu Chi after four decades. Fortunately, we found a good guide to take us there. The young man was fluent in English and knowledgeable in history, and not just the history of Vietnam. As we approached Cu Chi from the city, both sides of the road were covered with tall bamboo and green trees. I asked our guide if they were rubber trees. He smiled and nodded. In between, there were fields and nurseries of orchids. Vietnam is one of the leading suppliers of these exotic flowers to Japan.

Our young guide was the son of a farmer who had a small piece of land on which he grew black pepper. Our guide and his brother spent three months of the year helping their parents on the farm. Vietnam is overtaking India as the leading exporter of black pepper.

Could this green environment possibly be the Cu Chi of dust and large craters of forty years earlier? Groups of young European and Australian tourists were making their way to recreated tunnels which had once been the military base of the Viet Cong. They saw the hospitals and kitchens, and the individual underground facilities in which the Viet Cong had operated during the war, all of which had been recreated for public viewing. What they did not see and could not have imagined was the complete devastation of Cu Chi, which was ingrained in my memory from my visit there immediately after the war.

The delta of the Mekong, one of the longest rivers of Asia, has turned into a large producer of rice, which is not only the staple food of Vietnam, but also one of its biggest exports. This nation, which had defeated a superpower and its sophisticated war technology on the strength of its bicycles and its determination, has with the same determination been providing welfare to its people.

Salaam Vietnam!

4

New Delhi, 1979

Something unexpected and dramatic happened in May 1979. A pot which had been simmering boiled over. This was during the time when Atal Bihari Vajpayee was Minister for External Affairs and Jagat Mehta was Foreign Secretary. All the forty women officers in the Foreign Service received a letter from the Foreign Secretary urging them to choose between their career and their family. The letter said that it was to convey a 'warning' from the Foreign Minister to women officers that they should not ask for 'preferential treatment'. It said that there were seven husband-and-wife couples in the Service who sought postings, if not at the same place then close by, so that family life was not disrupted. When conveying this stern 'warning', it did not occur to the Minister, the Foreign Secretary, or the Head of Administration (S. K. Singh) that the letter should also have been sent to the male spouses (among the seven couples), who were equally responsible for causing administrative discomfort to the Ministry. The letter complained that women officers asked for favours like postings in comfortable 'A' stations, implying that men did not do so. The irony was that the letter itself was addressed to women officers serving in Conakry, Suva, Lagos, and Karachi, none of which was a comfortable 'A' posting.[1]

It was then and perhaps still is (I hope to a less extent now) taken for granted that working women were 'eating their cake and having it too'. They had the pleasure of family life and, in addition, they had a job outside the home. How unfair of them! Meanwhile, men have always combined the pleasures of having a family with having a job, which has been regarded as normal, and they have not been resented for 'eating their cake and having it too'.

The Foreign Secretary clarified in his three-page long letter that 'the intention is not to insist on resignation from the Foreign Service when lady members get married'. He was referring to a rule which had been followed years earlier. His own wife had had to resign from the Service when she married him. Subsequently, resignations were not demanded, but women had to get 'permission' before they got married. Men did not have to do that. Jagat Mehta's letter said that 'the ministry could go back to demanding resignation from women officers'. This bomb, which was served to all the women officers in this letter of 'warning', got an equally explosive response from the women, who demanded that the letter be withdrawn because it was downright discriminatory. It violated the Constitution of India, which gave equality to women.

There was in those days just one journalist who used to take up issues relating to gender justice. She was Rami Chhabra, a columnist in *The Indian Express*. I did not know her, but on my way home one day, I knocked on the door of her elegant house. I remember her reaction after she read the letter from the Foreign Secretary and then our rejoinder to it. She turned to me and asked very seriously, 'Are you sure you want to make this public? You might be asking for trouble. Have you thought of that?'

Beginning with her, the issue was given wide coverage. Journalists from all newspapers began asking questions. Many of them, irrespective of what they wrote, largely held the prejudiced view that women wanted to eat their cake and have it too. One of our own women colleagues in the Foreign Service strongly objected to having had the letter served to her. Arundhati Ghose said that she did not belong to the 'problem creating females' because she was not married. As for our men colleagues in the Foreign Service, most of them were tight-lipped. Prakash Shah 'offered' to take up the matter 'appropriately' with the Foreign Secretary on our 'behalf'. Did he really think that women were so incapable of talking on the subject that they needed a male lawyer to take up the issue with the Foreign Secretary? In short, there was confusion on many levels, which might even seem funny in hindsight now.

Some of us, on the other hand, also sought support from women IAS (Indian Administrative Service) officers. Here, we met with disappointment. My own batchmates in the Administrative Service were reluctant to even engage in a discussion on the issue of gender discrimination. One of them, whose husband was also in the IAS, frankly admitted that if she came out against gender discrimination in the Foreign Service, she might face problems at the time of her next posting. Somewhere there lurked a feeling among women officers that they were not quite equal and certainly vulnerable, so it was better to remain silent and invisible.

There were some very senior IAS officers like Anna Malhotra, who was scathing in her criticism of the Ministry. In an informal get-together of women officers, she broached the subject of double standards in our homes. Once, after dinner, early in her marriage, her husband had asked her, 'Don't you know how to make any other type of pudding?' To this, she had asked him in return, 'And how many puddings can you make?' Along with the laughter that followed her remarks tumbled out similar instances which others present had stashed away in their own silent dark corners. In that sense, Jagat Mehta's letter to women officers acted as a catalyst, which set in motion questions at many levels, both in offices and homes.

Our rejoinder to the Foreign Secretary evoked quite a commotion in the establishment. Although the Foreign Secretary's letter was not officially withdrawn, after the storm which followed it, the issue raised by it was silently buried. The formal burial of 'seeking resignation from women officers' had to wait till the end of a legal battle which the Government of India was fighting with C. B. Muthamma, the first woman IFS (Indian Foreign Service) officer of the 1948 batch, who had filed a petition in the Supreme Court alleging gender discrimination in the Service, of which she was a victim.

Muthamma was the topper of her batch and her record in the Service had been outstanding. Yet she was denied promotion to the senior-most grade, Grade-1, purely on grounds of gender bias and hostility. I was associated closely with her case even before she decided to file the petition, and had accompanied her to discussions with lawyers about the pros and cons of filing a petition.

I recall vividly the suspense with which I waited for the Judgment on the day it was expected to be delivered. She was at that time posted as Ambassador to The Hague. Around lunch time, I stepped into the room of T. P. Srinivasan, a colleague who was in the administration and would have received news about the Judgment. Even before I opened my mouth, he declared triumphantly that the Court had rejected Muthamma's petition. This came as a blow to me. Somehow, I was not convinced and wanted to lay my hands on the Judgment, for which I went to see my friend and colleague, Meira Kumar (who later resigned from the IFS, joined the Congress Party, and became Speaker of the Lok Sabha). Meira's husband, who was working in the administration of the Supreme Court, procured a copy of the Judgment delivered by Justice Krishna Iyer. Far from rejecting the petition, the Judge had made a strong and scathing indictment of the government; in his Judgment, he had chastised the government for its 'misogynist rules and blatant gender bias'.

At the heart of his Judgment, Justice Krishna Iyer said:

> What is more manifest as misogynist in the Foreign Service is the persistence of two rules which have been extracted in the petition. Rules 8(2) of the Indian Foreign Service (conduct and discipline) Rules 1961, unblushingly reads .... At any time after marriage, a woman member of the service may be required to resign from service if the government is satisfied that her family life and domestic commitments are likely to come in the way of her due and efficient discharge of her duties as a member of the service.

This rule was indeed the basis of the letter addressed by the Foreign Secretary to all women officers.

The Judge went on to say that 'discrimination against women in traumatic transparency is found in this rule'. He also said, 'If the family and domestic commitments of a woman member of the service is likely to come in the way of the efficient discharge of duties, a similar situation may well arise in the case of a male member.' We had said the same thing in our rejoinder to the letter of the Foreign Secretary.

The Judgment was equally scathing in observing the violation of Articles 14 and 16 of the Indian Constitution by Foreign Service rules. It said: '... it is a sad reflection on the distance between Constitution and law in action.'

While the Court proceedings were going on, Muthamma had been promoted. But justice was not done to her. Referring to this, Justice Krishna Iyer said:

> The central government states that although the petitioner was not found meritorious enough for promotion some months ago, she has been found to be good now, has been upgraded .... During the interval of some months before her first and second evaluations, some officers who were junior to her had become senior.

The Judgment recommended that 'her case with particular focus on seniority deserves a review vis-à-vis those junior to her who have been promoted in the interval of some months. The sense of injustice rankles and should be obliterated.' This recommendation of the Judgment proved impossible to be acted upon by a highly gender-biased government. The sense of injustice still rankles.

In order to rectify the falsehood being circulated by the Ministry that Muthamma's petition had been rejected by the Supreme Court, I was able with the help of sympathetic colleagues to get cyclostyled copies made of the Judgment of Justice Iyer, and had it distributed as widely as possible. Rami Chhabra wrote a long column on it in *The Indian Express*, which reached Muthamma by diplomatic bag.

I received a frantic telex message from her asking me why I had not sent her a copy of the Judgment. Muthamma's name had been left out in my list. On my part, I had taken it for granted that her lawyer would telex it to her on the day that it was delivered. All I could do at this late stage was to make sure that the next weekly diplomatic bag to The Hague carried to Muthamma the Supreme Court Judgment on her petition. The irony is that she was the last one to receive it.

After reading it and getting news of it from others who had received it before she had, Muthamma wrote me a letter expressing her fear and concern about the price which she expected would be extracted from me for sticking my neck out. The fact is that this whole episode only strengthened my friendship with Muthamma, which was a reward for me.

Justice Krishna Iyer's Judgment gave a formal and befitting burial to the Foreign Secretary's letter of warning to women officers that the government was ever ready to demand their resignation. Another refreshing outcome of the commotion created by the Foreign Secretary's letter and our rejoinder to it, followed by Justice Krishna Iyer's indictment of the blatant gender bias practised by the government, was that I received two unknown visitors who infused a new element into my routine-bound life. This was Subhadra Butalia, a feminist activist, and her young daughter Urvashi, who later made a name for herself as a writer, humanist, and feminist publisher. Subhadra was fighting a much bigger battle against the scourge of dowry deaths, which were rampant at that time.

Hardly a week passed between reported cases of the beating, burning, and killing of young women for not bringing the expected amounts of dowry. Subhadra and her small group used every means to raise awareness about domestic oppression and dowry killings. They would perform street plays. Subhadra composed songs. She sang and played the *dholak* (a two-headed Indian hand-drum). Her powerful voice and catchy music attracted crowds, and her group enacted the violent scenes which were everyday occurrences. The street plays were followed by interactions with the audience. Her dedication was complete and flawless, all the more so because she did not crave publicity.

Some of us from the Foreign Service (Meera Shankar, Parvati Sen, and I) and from the Administrative Service (Kalyani Choudhuri of the West Bengal cadre) joined Subhadra, Urvashi, and their friends to form a women's group called 'Karmika'. We held regular meetings, either in Subhadra's house or mine. Over time, we moved from awareness of dowry deaths to cases of rape. Subhadra's help was being sought by victims of dowry and rape cases. The inadequacy of legal remedies to fight gender injustice was part of her life and soon became part of the focus of our group. It was shocking to hear from the then chairman of the Law Commission, when we went to meet him, that the Indian Evidence Act did not recognise the statements given by a rape victim as 'sufficient legal evidence'. If she is robbed, a woman's evidence is counted, but when she is raped, her statement is not sufficient to be treated as evidence.

We began meeting with representatives of women's groups to discuss the need to change the Evidence Act, which was crassly unjust to victims of rape. There came a stage when, after almost a year of preparation, 'Karmika' called a meeting of women's groups, which included front organisations of almost all political parties from the Right to the Left and the Centre, on this issue with the purpose of building a consensus to change the Evidence Act. The meeting was very well-attended. The room in Subhadra's house could just about accommodate the participants packed in it. I presided over the meeting, which began with Subhadra explaining the issue clearly, as had been done for us by the chairman of the Law Commission. One by one the representatives of organisations of political parties expressed their opposition to changing the Evidence Act. Clearly, they were voicing the opinions of the political parties that they were representing. Their gender identity found no expression over their political identity. It was buried too deep to make an appearance in conflict with party lines. Irrespective of Right, Left, or Centre, male identity dominated the discussion. I was very disappointed. A few months after this, I was to leave for my posting to Mexico. Subhadra had, it seemed to me, expected this turn of events and was not one to give up. She was not only much older than I, but she was also patient and much wiser.

Alone she plodded along, working for the cause. Several decades later, the Evidence Act was changed. Subhadra Butalia finally won the battle in 2013 although she was no longer there to witness it. The evidence of rape victims was made legally admissible.[2]

In 1985, I came to Delhi on home leave and found that Subhadra had opened an office to provide free legal aid to women in need of it. One of my school friends was a beneficiary of it. Subhadra's enthusiasm and refusal to give up even when she found herself alone is still an inspiration to those who knew her. I last met her at a get-together organised by Muthamma in 2001 to celebrate the appointment of Chukila Iyer as the first woman Foreign Secretary, a position that had been unfairly denied to Muthamma almost twenty-five years earlier.

Notes

1. Postings are in categories of A*, A, B, C, and C* according to living standards. The 'A*' postings are the most sought after with the best living standards, like London, New York, Washington, etc. The 'B' and 'C' postings are those where living conditions are less comfortable, and 'C*' postings are where living conditions are really difficult.

2. In criminal cases, a First Information Report (FIR) is recorded by the police and may be provided by any person who has knowledge of the commission of the offence. An FIR is not under oath and does not constitute evidence as per the law. In rape cases, the courts generally looked for evidence in the medical report, or statements of witnesses. This makes it difficult for victims of rape to successfully convict the accused as the medical examination may not have been conducted, and there are no witnesses to the offence.

There are judgments on how a rape victim's testimony is to be evaluated. From the 1990s onwards, jurisprudence has moved away from looking for proof in terms of medical evidence or other proof to corroborate the victim's testimony. These judgments have held that the sole testimony of the victim (prosecutrix), if credible, is sufficient, and medical evidence is not mandatory in cases of rape. They hold that a rape victim should be treated akin to an injured witness, or even on a higher footing, and should not be treated as an accomplice (as was the case earlier). Some relevant judgments are reproduced below.

The Supreme Court, in *State of Punjab vs. Gurmit Singh* AIR (1996) SC 1993, held:

> Why should the evidence of a girl or a woman who complains of rape or sexual molestation, be viewed with doubt, disbelief or suspicion? The Court while appreciating the evidence of a prosecutrix may look for some assurance of her statement

> to satisfy its judicial conscience, since she is a witness who is interested in the outcome of the charge levelled by her, but there is no requirement of law to insist upon corroboration of her statement to base conviction of an accused. (Para 8)

Therefore, the sole testimony of the victim is sufficient to lead to conviction, provided the court finds her testimony to be reliable. The Judgment given in *Gurmit Singh* has been reiterated in numerous other cases of the higher judiciary.

In 2013, following the gang-rape and murder of a young physiotherapy student in New Delhi, who was named Nirbhaya (the fearless one) in the media, amendments were made to criminal law. In an offence punishable under Section 354, 354A, 354B, 354C, 354D, sub-section (1) or (2), Section 376, 376A, 376B, 376C, 376D, 376E, or 509 of the Indian Penal Code (IPC), it is now compulsory for a Magistrate to record the statement of the survivor under Section 164 of the Code of Criminal Procedure 1973. If the victim is suffering from temporary or permanent mental or physical disability, her statement before the Magistrate shall be taken to be the examination-in-chief (which means that her statement made before the Magistrate will also be deemed to have been made in court).

5

National Defence College, Delhi, 1980

The National Defence College (NDC) in Delhi, which is located opposite the Birla House on Tees January Marg where Mahatma Gandhi was assassinated, provides the highest course of study for the senior members of the defence forces. Stretching over a year, it covers subjects of social, political, and strategic interest. Apart from senior members of the defence services, it used to have place for two officers, one each from the Administrative and the Foreign Service. I was delegated by the Ministry of External Affairs (MEA) to be a student officer at the course in 1980. It was going to be a complete change from working in a territorial division of the Ministry and that was attractive in itself, although I had no idea what to expect from it.

As it turned out, it was a novel and exciting exposure. In addition to lectures by distinguished speakers on various subjects, it involved the writing of a research paper by each student officer on a subject of the individual's choice. This was the time when rumblings had started in Poland that a resistance movement (led by 'Solidarity', the first independent labour union in a Soviet-bloc country) against a Soviet-backed communist regime was gaining strength. Writing a paper on a popular movement against a strong centralised government was something I found most interesting and educative. It prepared me for opting for more such work later in the Policy Planning Division of the Ministry at the end of this course.

During the year, small teams of students toured some parts of the country to get an idea of the situation on the ground as distinct from the figures and pictures drawn by official agencies. I joined the group which travelled to Odisha, Andhra Pradesh, and Tamil Nadu. Similarly, we toured and explored some regions abroad. I was in a group of very senior officers, most of them of the rank of Brigadier General, who toured Algeria, Libya, Saudi Arabia, and Burma. None of these countries were multi-party democracies. They were all run by military governments. Seeing them along with officials of the armed forces made it all the more interesting.

I recall that at the completion of the course, when I returned to the MEA, I wrote a strong note to the administration in favour of instituting in-house training courses for officers in the Foreign Service of the type that officers in the defence forces are required to undergo at various stages in their careers. I am not sure if anyone other than I ever read that note.

Among the lectures that we heard by distinguished people, the one I recall vividly was addressed by Verghese Kurien, the founder of Amul Milk Cooperative, the leading success story of independent India. Student officers were encouraged to suggest names of speakers, and I suggested that Dr Kurien be invited. My interest in hearing him went back to the time when, during my years as a young Undersecretary at the Ministry, the then President of the Soviet Union, Leonid Brezhnev, visited India. Those were the heady days of close relations between Delhi and Moscow. Brezhnev had evinced an interest in visiting Anand in Gujarat where Amul's Cooperative Milk plant was located. He wanted to personally meet Dr Kurien. As per the President's wishes, a night's stay in Anand was programmed for him along with a meeting with the founder of Amul.

Dr Kurien's lecture was not devoid of suspense. The story of milk production with the involvement of more than a million small producers, who became equal stakeholders in a countrywide project and made India the world's biggest milk producer, was narrated by him almost as well as it was screened in Shyam Benegal's film *Manthan* (1976). He also gave an account of the ongoing project 'Dhara', which sought to bring edible oil production into a similar cooperative involving very large numbers of small oil-seed producers as stakeholders. At the end of the lecture, I had the chance to ask him the question which had nagged me for so long: What had President Brezhnev's meeting with him been about? The answer was short and to the point. The Soviet President had heard of the success of Amul's cooperative model. He had asked if Dr Kurien thought that India had the time to develop slowly on the lines of Amul's success story. Dr Kurien had answered that he knew of no better model than that of involving people as stakeholders in development like in a cooperative.

It is another matter that over time, even Dr Kurien could not prevent corporate houses in their aggressive search for markets from entering what had once been an exclusively cooperative scheme, involving the smallest producer as an equal stakeholder.

As I have related, we travelled in small groups as part of the course to different parts of the country to see for ourselves the ground realities as they were. I retain a very vivid memory of the visit to Odisha, during which we visited a Buddhist temple built with Japanese assistance not far from Bhubaneswar. The temple was at a height and provided a clear view of the Daya River below. King Ashoka was supposed to have been horror-struck at the massive number of dead bodies he saw on the banks of Daya, which had turned into a river of blood after his great victory in the Battle of Kalinga. He is said to have converted to Buddhism and adopted the *dharma* of nonviolence soon after. Here, I was confronted by a beggar. She was an old woman whose shrivelled skin and bones were barely covered by the rags she was wearing. She could have been one of the survivors of the Kalinga war. For her, nothing had changed.

In fact, nothing had changed for the people who lived in the forests and were being counted as Scheduled Tribes, in the hilly regions where they continued to live as they had been living for centuries. The hills and forests are their life and their gods. However, a lot has been happening to them and to their environment since my first visit to Odisha in 1980 with the NDC. Large and valuable deposits of iron-ore and bauxite, among other minerals, have been discovered under the forests where they live. National and multi-national companies have entered a race to exploit these treasures, which has led to intense resistance in some areas by people fighting against being displaced and uprooted from their livelihoods and their lives, which are intertwined with the forests, hills, and rivers. In some exceptional cases, the companies have had to bow to the strong resistance they have encountered, although it would be premature to say that they have given up. As of 2016,[1] the Niyamgiri hill range, the seat of the tribal god Niyam Raja, has evaded being dynamited for bauxite mining, as part of a project by state government-owned Odisha Mining Corporation and Vedanta[2] Ltd. for the latter's aluminium refinery in a neighbouring area. Similarly, a strong resistance, largely from the betel vine farmers of Jagatsinghpur district, has prevented POSCO (Pohang Iron and Steel Company, formerly),[3] a South Korean company, from taking over their fertile agricultural land for iron-ore mining, despite every effort by the Central and the state government. In fact, the latter had entered into an agreement with the company and given approval for the mining and export of iron-ore in return for a very large foreign investment by POSCO. At US$ 12 billion, it was reported to have been the largest foreign direct investment (FDI) offer that India had received till then. POSCO exited the steel project in 2017.

In Hyderabad, our group had a meeting with Chenna Reddy, the then Chief Minister of Andhra Pradesh. We expected him to acquaint us with his achievements and future plans. His heavy-weight personality was matched by a heavy-weight gold chain around his neck. Every finger of the Chief Minister had precious stone-studded rings. While his guests were offered cold water in glass tumblers, the Chief Minister drank out of a silver-and-gold tumbler. The development of his state matched this image with some precision. The newly constructed secretariat building resembled an ornate palace of a maharaja.

The Defence Ministry's research and organisation centre, the Defence Research and Development Organisation (DRDO) in Hyderabad, was then in the process of making electronic devices. Funds to that organisation had not yet dwindled to a trickle like in the later years of economic reforms. Scientists shared with us their enthusiasm and work with pride.

The year 1980 witnessed two political events of some significance. The national elections brought Indira Gandhi back to power within three years after a massive and humiliating defeat at the hands of a united opposition of largely Right-wing parties called Janata Dal. Shortly after her return as Prime Minister, her son Sanjay Gandhi, who was believed to exercise a lot of influence over her, and who had allegedly become an extra-constitutional authority, died in a plane crash. I heard of the plane crash at the petrol pump on my way to NDC.

Officers of the NDC had a meeting with the Prime Minister a few months later in her office. She addressed the meeting and handled questions without a trace of the political wilderness from which she had emerged after three years, and of the personal tragedy that she had faced just three months earlier.

Algeria

Algeria was the first Arab country, among others, that our team, comprising largely of senior Brigadier-ranking officers, visited. As it happened, our aircraft landed on the runway at the airport of Algiers moments after a massive earthquake had disoriented the capital city. Had it landed at the precise moment when the quake had struck, it might not have been able to land in one piece. Sitting in the plane, we felt the tremors which follow such phenomena. The crew and our hosts were in a state of shock, as was the city of Algiers. With some delay, we finally arrived at our hotel, which was not far from the sea. The large white building had undergone a jolt which was evident from the many cracks in the walls. After the first tremors of the earthquake, the aftershock was trivial and very familiar to those coming from Delhi.

Algiers faced regular water shortage. Water scarcity in those days was part of the definition of being 'underdeveloped'. In course of time, the 'underdeveloped' countries changed the situation by calling themselves 'developing' countries. It sounded more respect-able, although the water problem continued.

The military government and the elite of the country were deeply conscious and proud of the armed struggle against the colonial power of France which had, after eight years of a brutal war, successfully led to the independence of Algeria in 1962. A country of (at that time) nine million people is estimated to have lost 1.5 million people in that war of independence. Those who had sided with the colonial rulers at the time were later severely punished. It was natural that the heroes of the anti-colonial war should take over the reins of power in the newly independent country. Leaders like Ahmed Ben Bella and Abdelaziz Bouteflika, who had led the war, were among them. The army was instrumental in liberating Algeria from French rule in 1962. Ben Bella served as the first President of Algeria till 1965. Later, Bouteflika was President of the country for twenty years (1999–2019), despite his age and weak health. This is not unusual. In India, the freedom movement was largely led by lawyers who took over the reins of power when freedom arrived. The profession of law has dominated the Indian political scene from the beginning, and continues to do so even today. Among our leaders during the independence struggle, Subhash Chandra Bose was one of the exceptions. He was not a lawyer.

When we visited Algeria in 1980, there were no signs of resistance to the military regime. There was much hope in accelerated economic development because rich gas reserves were being discovered in the country. It was not till the 1990s that Algerians began to demand a participatory multi-party democracy. The ruling government came close to holding elections, but withdrew in the face of strong Islamic religious forces which had begun to dominate the call for electoral politics. Like in Turkey, in Algeria, too, the army has been the guardian of secularism. It has tried to keep religion from dominating politics. However, the situation in Turkey has been changing in recent years and place has been made for Islamic religious domination. Politics dominated by 'cultural nationalism' is unmistakeably an evolving trend around the world. In Turkey, this trend was resisted for many decades till Atatürk's army began to be viewed, especially in the 1990s, as an 'elitist' force, which the large majority did not identify with. Much earlier, a similar resistance by the majority against the elitist rule of the Shah in Iran broke all bounds in the Islamic Revolution of 1979. The Shah's regime had enjoyed the strong support of the United States of America. Perhaps because of that, and also the glaring and growing inequality between the ruling establishment and the vast majority of the people, cultural nationalism swept over the country as a very strong force. Cultural nationalism flourishes in majoritarianism. Parliamentary democracy, which favours the party that gets elected by the largest number of votes, also provides the best soil for nurturing it.

One of the most memorable experiences that I recall from the visit to Algeria was an excursion to Tipasa. Situated on the shores of the blue Mediterranean Sea about 60–70 kilometres from Algiers, it is an archaeological site of Roman ruins. The centuries-old, long brown columns of a once Roman temple rise from an orange and yellow beach where the sky meets the blue sea. The approach to Tipasa is through olive groves and green forests. Nature has created remarkable beauty in Tipasa, which leaves an indelible mark on visitors to the site. Some years later, I read an essay by Albert Camus titled 'Return to Tipasa', in which the Nobel Laureate had done justice to it. Camus was born and brought up in French Algeria. In 1952, after having lived through the horrors of World War II and deeply disturbed by questions of injustice and morality, he visited Tipasa again and this is what he wrote:

> I discovered once more at Tipasa that one must keep intact in oneself a freshness, a cool wellspring of joy, love the day that escapes injustice, and return to combat having won that light. Here I recaptured the former beauty, a young sky, and I measured my luck, realizing at last that in the worst years of our madness the memory of that sky had never left me. This was what in the end had kept me from despairing. I had always known that the ruins of Tipasa were younger

than our new constructions or our bomb damage .... In the
middle of winter I at last discovered that there was in me an
invincible summer.[4]

I recall that I was not alone and that most of us were moved by the
natural beauty and the ancient remains on the seashore of Tipasa.
On the return journey in the bus, someone broke the silence that
had fallen over us by whispering aloud that such natural beauty was
very rare.

The city of Algiers is strikingly white, which is the dominant
colour of its buildings and homes. In 1980, it was unusual for
someone from India to see TV antennae in the sky over Algiers'
slums. This was yet to happen in our homeland where TV, which
meant Doordarshan, had not yet reached urban slums.

There was an ongoing cooperation between the governments
of India and Algeria in the field of education. A substantial number
of teachers of mathematics and English language from government
schools in India were sent to teach in Algerian schools. We met
many of them, who considered themselves fortunate to have had
the opportunity of exposure to a new culture and to work in a
friendly and hospitable environment. Later, we were to find more
instances of South–South cooperation (which was the name given
to cooperation between poor and developing countries in the global
South) going beyond the field of education in Libya. In today's
globalised, corporate world, even the memory of those heady days
of South–South cooperation has disappeared, like drops of water in
the Sahara Desert.

The Sahara Desert comprises almost three-quarters of
Algeria's land. Most of this area is not liveable, so the population is
concentrated near the coastline of the Mediterranean Sea. One of
the souvenirs which I brought back with me from that visit was a
desert rose, which still sits on my desk. This is one of the wonders
of nature: a flower created out of sand by strong desert winds. This
one on my table is a dull orange colour. It has stood the test of many
years and looks as fresh today as it did in 1980.

Libya

Geographically, Libya and Algeria are close neighbours. Most of their land is desert, but under the Libyan Desert sands are big oil reserves. The currents of history which flowed through these deserts distinguished the two countries and gave them very different characters. The Roman Empire first and the Ottoman Empire later left archaeological remains on the coastal regions of both countries. Later, Algeria became a prized French colony. For a short period, Libya turned into a colony of Italy, but reverted to a kingdom in 1943. The country came into prominence after the takeover of political power by a young leader in a *coup d'état* in 1969. Colonel Muammar Gaddafi was only twenty-seven years old then, and had a great advantage because large reserves of petroleum were discovered in Libya soon after he came to power.

We arrived in Tripoli, the capital of Libya, from Algiers. As we drove from the airport to the city, I was taken aback to see rows of two and three-storeyed flats which were reminiscent of Indian Public Works Department (PWD) constructions. It looked as though the residential flats of Delhi's Rama Krishna Puram had been physically transferred to the Libyan capital. The reason for this was revealed later.

Our team had the advantage of a background briefing from Narendra Singh Sarila, our then Ambassador in Libya, who briefed us under a shady tree in the garden of his residence. Many years later, he published a book called *The Shadow of the Great Game: The Untold Story of India's Partition* (2005), which is one of the best books on the subject, written after extensive research spread over many years in the archives in London.

Our team was looked after by the armed forces of Libya and accommodated in their prestigious guest house. We were also told that I was the first woman to step into that exclusively male military domain. Our Ambassador's wife came to visit me to see the sort of privileges I was being given. I cannot remember if her visit came before or after this incident at night. I found that my room had a glass wall overlooking a yard. At night, a piercing search light was directed right into the room, which made it impossible to sleep. To avoid the strong light, I tried to pull down the screens, but it proved to be an impossible task for my non-military hands, despite my best efforts. Since there was no telephone in the room, I had to step out to find someone to help pull the screens down. I opened the door and almost fell over a six-foot tall man. Finding someone standing within inches of the door shocked me. What was this man doing right on my doorstep? It took me a few moments to recover. He asked me if I needed anything and, at my request, obliged by pulling down the screens. Having been saved from the piercing search light and after recovering from the shock—which took some time—I finally went to sleep. It looked as though, without my knowledge, I had been provided with a bodyguard. Later, it looked like I was under some sort of surveillance. At the end of the first day, I was politely asked why I was not eating properly, why I was eating only fruit. The fact is that the fruit, especially the grapes and dates, tasted very good. The food was tasteless and almost synthetic. But so as not to be misunderstood by those who were deputed to keep a close watch, I felt forced to eat at least a little of everything.

On the bedside table in my room, I found a copy of *The Green Book* (1975). Like Mao's *The Little Red Book* (or *Quotations from Chairman Mao Tse-tung*) (1964), Gaddafi had his political and social philosophy inscribed in his *Green Book*, which was regarded as the Bhagavad Gita or the Bible of his country. Gaddafi debunked all forms of elected, representational government. The instruments of governments the world over are dictatorial, even if they claim to be democratic, he said. The only democratic way was for people to run their own affairs in local committees and through locally run secretariats. As for making laws of governance, he was of the view that it is not for men to make laws. Laws are grounded in tradition and religion. Anything outside tradition and religion is illogical and invalid. This view, which has come to be known as cultural nationalism, has today been gaining prevalence in many countries. In some, it is being accommodated within a parliamentary system.

Gaddafi's solution for economic problems was socialism. The ownership of property is not to be in the hands of an individual, family, or tribe. Ownership of property is to be collective, he said.

Gaddafi combined his notion of socialism, which included the fair distribution of national wealth, with religious nationalism. He was in favour of gender equality, he said, although how that is to be combined and accommodated with tradition and religion was left unsaid.

Nationalism, according to Gaddafi, was another name for religion or tradition. If this factor is diluted by minorities demanding their own rights, then the nation would be destroyed, he believed.

Libya had the advantage not only of vast oil reserves, but also of a relatively thin population of just around two million people. Gaddafi's socialism provided the distribution of a share of petroleum revenues among the people. Special shops were run by the government outside the bazaars, where imported goods were sold at reasonable prices. I remember buying from one of these shops a toy train, which was a thundering success with my daughters.

Educational institutions, including medical colleges, were opened to which, under South–South cooperation, the Government of India also provided experts, teachers, and doctors. Gaddafi had promised that he would provide free housing to the people. It was in the execution of this project that Indian (PWD) architects created colonies like Delhi's Rama Krishna Puram in Tripoli, the first sight of which had left me speechless.

South–South cooperation was not a mere platitude in Gaddafi's Libya. His foreign policy was marked by financial and moral assistance to what were regarded as rebel nations and organisations. These included Fidel Castro's Cuba, Yasser Arafat's Palestine Liberation Organization (PLO), Daniel Ortega's Nicaragua, and Nelson Mandela's African National Congress (ANC). It is said that one of Mandela's grandsons was named Gaddafi in appreciation of the enthusiastic support given by the Libyan leader to Mandela's cause. To add to this, Libya purchased arms and weaponry from the Soviet Union and France. Gaddafi gave short shrift to the American government. American oil companies, on the other hand, were given big contracts in Libya, on the best terms, it was reported.

For all his popularity, the Libyan leader's whereabouts were a closely guarded secret. Our delegation did not get the chance to meet the leader, although the hope of such a meeting was kept alive till the last moment. On one of our excursions to an archaeological site, we had to make an unscheduled diversion. It was whispered that probably the leader was returning from where we were heading.

Unlike Algiers, Tripoli was not an attractive city. Among the many Indians working in Libya, there was a feeling that immigrant workers were looked down upon by a people who had suddenly come upon oil wealth.

Gaddafi's contempt for America and American antipathy towards him escalated over time. Three decades later, Gaddafi and Libya paid a heavy price for standing up to the superpower. While Saddam Hussein was killed and Iraq destroyed on the pretext of his possessing weapons of mass destruction, Libya was bombed and totally crushed by NATO (North Atlantic Treaty Organization) powers, in attacks exclusively from the air till the country was shattered beyond recognition. Gaddafi was brutally murdered. This was all done in the name of instituting democracy in these countries.

In the Middle East, the United Nations (UN) has acted like a pliable tool of the most dominant military power. The UN-approved team led by Hans Blix, former chief of the International Atomic Energy Agency (IAEA), clearly stated in his report to the UN that there was no evidence of weapons of mass destruction in Iraq. The world watched on TV screens as he said this, but the excuse was still maintained. Fifteen years later, Iraq is still recovering from the destruction of a war which was based on a lie. As for the attack on Libya, the UN was sidelined. NATO powers wanted to get rid of Gaddafi. Once again, the world watched as this was achieved by concentrated bombings, which killed the people and destroyed their land. Did the people of Libya not count? In hindsight, Gaddafi's Libya appears like a mirage in the desert. Perhaps what counted were the rich oil reserves in Iraq and in Libya, which had given confidence and, as it turned out, a false sense of independence to the leaders of these countries.

On our way back, we made a short stopover in Saudi Arabia. On arriving in Riyadh, at the immigration counter of the airport, I was asked to point out which member of the delegation was my husband. When I said 'none', there was a little commotion. Till that moment, I had not realised how dangerous a single woman is considered in the heavily armed Royal Kingdom. I was not going to be allowed to enter the country. As it happened, the Indian Ambassador had come to the airport to receive us. His intervention softened the stance of the immigration officers. Since I was part of a high-level military delegation and was neither going to be on my own nor staying longer than a few hours in the country, and the Indian Ambassador was taking full responsibility, they were prepared to allow me entry on the condition that the immigration authority would keep my passport with them till I left the Kingdom.

The esteem of our Ambassador soared higher in my eyes during a second incident at the customs counter, where he impressed me with his tactful and firm handling of an event. Alcohol is viewed with suspicion there, although it is not considered as dangerous as a single woman. Bottles of whiskey in the baggage of the senior delegates were about to be confiscated when Ambassador Chhattwal declared with authority that those bottles contained orange juice. To stress his point, he offered the customs official one of the bottles. No passports were confiscated. The official accepted the bottle of orange juice offered to him and we were allowed to enter the Kingdom of Saudi Arabia.

The short halt in Riyadh and a drive through the city was unimpressive, except for a massive, newly constructed but abandoned building. What made that building special, we were told, was that its architects had not made any provision for the parking of cars, which was why it could not be used. Several years later, one encountered the same situation in the centre of the city of Calcutta, where air-conditioned markets, the precursors of malls, were coming up without any provision for car parking. The only difference was that the markets in Calcutta were not abandoned and were allowed to freely add to the existing overcrowded chaos. There were no traffic rules, much less parking spaces. Moreover, there were many poor rickshaw pullers; it was altogether quite chaotic.

At the time of departure, I was handed my passport. We were flying on the national air carrier of Saudi Arabia. The crew and air hostesses were all British. Since this was the month of Ramzan, passengers were not offered any refreshments, not even water. I was carrying with me, in my hand baggage, juicy dates still hanging on their stems, to bring back to Delhi. These were enjoyed by all of us on the flight, including the air hostesses.

We had barely returned to Delhi when war broke out between Iraq and Iran. Saddam Hussein had the backing, motivation, and full support of the United States (US), which provided him the latest weaponry in unaccounted numbers. This war continued for seven long years, during which it caused enormous damage to life and resources in Iran. However, although it disrupted life, it did not succeed in breaking the country and its morale. Iran gradually found its feet again.

By 2003, Saddam Hussein had turned from a dependable friend and ally of the US to an evil despot. The people of Iraq deserved democracy and to save them from a despot, a war was declared on them. Libya, too, had to be saved from its despotic ruler. Then came the turn of Syria; it too deserved democracy, and so a war continues to destroy the lives of its people even today. After the destruction of large parts of West Asia by NATO powers, increasing numbers of refugees from these countries have been trying to find shelter and livelihood in Turkey and European countries, where they are not welcome. Anti-immigration sentiments have become central to politics in Europe as a result.

With the financial backing of Saudi Arabia, a large army of uprooted young men has been created to restore Islamic supremacy in the region. This newly created Islamic State of Iraq and the Levant (ISIL) force has only added to the chaos. The political geography of a prosperous West Asia in 1980 has now been reduced to dust.

Burma

The last military-run country that our team visited was Burma (now called Myanmar). This journey to the East was like going back in time. The country had not yet entered the age of industrialisation. It looked like a large workforce, predominantly of women, was engaged in agriculture and in marketing the produce. Men were patient onlookers. The rest were engaged in fighting rebel minority communities in the west and the north of the country.

Burma was a country of vast green forests interrupted by white pagodas, which was very picturesque to behold. There were few cars on the roads of Rangoon and almost no traffic. The temples were very well kept from the outside. While the rest of our team went inside the big temple in Rangoon, I was politely kept out. I had been under the wrong impression that Buddhism was relatively more favourable to gender equality. In some of our own temples in South India, women are not allowed entry. In a much larger number of temples in the country, the entry of Dalits and foreigners is banned. Not all religions respect the notion of equality, which is a relatively new social concept yet to be accepted.

On a visit to Mandalay, the second largest town, we were told not to venture out on our own without armed escorts. The country was going through an upheaval of the sort we are familiar with in the Northeast of our own country, where minority communities have been asserting their independence through armed struggle against the forces of the State. Mandalay town had a deserted look. It seemed that people had run away, either to fight with the forces of the State or with one of the rebel minority groups, and left the town empty. The military regime certainly had its hands full.

Before leaving Rangoon, we paid a visit to the grave of Bahadur Shah Zafar, the last Mughal emperor, who was sent into exile in Rangoon by the British after the uprising against British rule in 1857 (which they had called a mutiny). Zafar spent his last years in isolation in Burma. His grave was in a graveyard which bore a wild look. The grave itself was uncared for and forgotten. It reminded me of a similar forgotten grave in Gwalior of the great singer Miyan Tansen, who had been one of the jewels in the court of Mughal emperor Akbar. That forgotten and forsaken grave breaks the heart of any music lover who takes the trouble of finding the resting place of the renowned singer.

Ten years later, the Government of India made a move to recognise Bahadur Shah Zafar and created a monument at the site of his grave. One wonders why it took so long to recognise the man who had been hailed as the leader of the 1857 uprising. Did the political class in India also support the British view that it was merely a mutiny?

Bahadur Shah Zafar is remembered less for having led the uprising in 1857 and more for the poems and ghazals which the poet-emperor had left behind. In one of his poems, he lamented that he could not find his final resting place among his loved ones.

Notes

1. *Business Standard*. 2016. 'Supreme Court quashes Odisha's plea on Niyamgiri', 6 May. Available at https://www.business-standard.com/article/current-affairs/supreme-court-quashes-odisha-s-plea-on-niyamgiri-116050601256_1.html (accessed June 2021).

2. *Business & Human Rights Resource Centre*. 2017. 'Vedanta Resources Lawsuit (re Dongria Kondh in Orissa)', 27 November. Available at https://www.business-humanrights.org/en/latest-news/vedanta-resources-lawsuit-re-dongria-kondh-in-orissa/(accessed June 2021).

3. *Scroll.in*. 2017. 'As Posco exits steel project, Odisha is left with thousands of felled trees and lost livelihoods', 22 March. Available at https://scroll.in/article/832463/as-posco-exits-steel-project-odisha-is-left-with-thousands-of-felled-trees-and-broken-job-promises (accessed June 2021).

4. Camus, Albert. 1991 [1955]. 'Return to Tipasa'. In A. Camus, *The Myth of Sisyphus and Other Essays*, Justin O'Brien (trans.), 193–204. USA: Vintage International.

6

Mexico City, 1983

In February 1983, I arrived in Mexico City along with my daughters—Rakhi, who was eight years old, and Meghna, who was six—to take up my post as Minister Counsellor at the Embassy. Amit arrived a few months later to take up a visiting professorship at El Colegio de México, which is a postgraduate university. After enrolling the children in school, we started taking lessons in Spanish. It seemed a relatively easier language to learn after Vietnamese. I have spent the first few months in every posting learning the local language. It is not possible to function without a minimum level of familiarity with the language and the history of the place. Throughout my career in the Foreign Service, I have a record of never being posted in an English-language country.

While we were struggling with Spanish grammar, Rakhi and Meghna were happily picking up the language at school and while playing with their many friends in the neighbourhood of Polanco, where we lived in the same compound as the Indian Embassy. Unlike myself at their age (I used to cry my way to school, which I hated), my daughters were always ready to catch their school bus. It seemed that the school bus driver turned the daily journey of going to and returning from school into a sort of excursion, which the children enjoyed. They would cheer him when he quarrelled on the road and they picked up swear words off the street as easily as catching balls. Through them, I became acquainted with such words as well.

After having acquired a sufficient 'feel' of the language, I went one Saturday to the large market downtown where I was told one could buy the best fish and meat. It was a gigantic market spread over a vast area; it was almost a town by itself. I made my way through crowds of people and a lot of dirt to reach the fish stalls, all the while being very conscious of the many eyes seeing a sari for the first time. I selected the fish and had it cut to my liking. Before packing it, the shopkeeper asked me if I wanted the head. I did not. But instead of saying 'I don't want the head', I said, 'I don't have one'. The '*No lo quiero*' (I do not want it) became '*No lo tengo*' (I do not have it). The wrong verb was out and the curious crowds roared with laughter. The fish market became a friendly place. I imagine that I became familiar as the señora without a head.

At that time, Mexico City was the world's largest and most populated city with twenty million inhabitants. A few decades earlier, it had been known as the region with the most transparent air. It was then decidedly a very attractive place—cool, green, and never too warm or too cold. This was before one quarter of the county's population moved to live in it, and the congestion of cars on its streets turned it into the world's most polluted city. I remember the astonishment of Karan Singh, a Member of Parliament (MP) and then chairman of the Indian Council for Cultural Relations (ICCR), when he visited Mexico. 'It is even bigger than Calcutta!' Dr Singh had exclaimed in disbelief.

Most underprivileged parts of the city suffered from a shortage of water and absence of sewage facilities. The rich localities had private swimming pools and tennis courts. Meghna had once commented, 'We are the poorest people on our street.' 'Why do you think so?' I had asked. 'Because all the houses on our street have swimming pools, except ours,' she had replied. She was very fond of swimming, which she had learnt and was enjoying in school.

Mexico (the country) boasted of the largest number of private jets. Its rich gentry had militias of their own. What had surprised me as a newcomer was to find that the price of petrol and Coca-Cola was less than the price of milk. As it happened, our arrival in Mexico had coincided with a currency crash. Within the next three years of our stay there, the Mexican peso kept tumbling. From an exchange rate of 12 pesos to US$ 1, it came down to 3,000 pesos to US$ 1.

The production of and illegal trade in narcotics had overtaken a once flourishing agricultural production. Gang wars and drug trafficking thrived, along with a song-and-dance culture. Every Sunday, the city squares had live music, to which people danced with abandon. Dancing was a shade more popular than going to church. Mexicans spent what they earned. I felt that for me, an Indian, the Latin American love for life, of living for this moment was an eye-opener, an education in itself. In India, we carry the burden of our traditions, religious and cultural. In addition, we carry the burden of wanting to leave an inheritance (preferably along with a house) for our children. This leaves us with little time and no inclination to savour life, beyond celebrating weddings and festivals with an increasingly greater show of wealth, jewellery, and louder music.

The Mexican elite largely consists of fair-skinned people of Spanish descent. The ruling elite has few 'Mestizos' in it, who are mixed offspring of the indigenous people and the Spanish colonisers. Their skin is not white. The indigenous people are still darker in colour. They are at the bottom of the social ladder and are called 'Indo', not to be confused with people from India, who are called 'Hindu'. Most of the local staff in the Indian Embassy were Mestizos. This included my secretary, Laura, who was indispensable to me in every difficult situation, a friend in all situations, and with whom I continue to correspond. My daughters turned to Ricardo, our handyman at the Embassy, for every problem. Once, when their doll had stopped crying, they went to him and Ricardo slapped the doll hard. She began to cry and Ricardo became a hero!

Rakhi was about ten years old when the starving children of Somalia made global news. The then most popular pop singer, Michael Jackson, wrote a hit song about the children of Somalia. Plump Meghna, who was often called *'gorda'* (fat), found an appropriate name for Rakhi: 'Somalia's daughter'. 'Rakhi looks like she does not get enough to eat,' she said. However, Rakhi was good at gymnastics and sports, in which she used to win prizes.

One day, to fetch the children, I had walked across the road to the corner where the school bus used to drop them. When the bus arrived, there was some commotion. Meghna got off the bus, crying out in excitement, 'Rakhi is a hero!' Rakhi stepped down from the bus with the entire bus shouting, 'Bravo Rakhi! Bravo Rakhi!' The bus driver said to me, *'Señora, su hija es preciosa'* (Madame, your daughter is precious). More 'Bravo Rakhi!' followed as the bus moved on. I held their hands as we crossed the road. Once out of the traffic area, I asked, 'What happened?' Meghna kept saying, 'Ma, Rakhi is a hero.' Rakhi was serious and silent. Finally, Meghna gave an account of the incident.

In the morning, as usual, they had boarded the bus and occupied their allotted seats. A little while later, one of the two Dutch boys (about sixteen and seventeen years old, tall and well-built, with blue eyes and blonde hair) who sat in the seats in front of them turned around and shouted accusingly at Rakhi, 'Black! Black! Black!' A little later, one of them turned around again and repeated it, this time louder and more forcefully, 'Black, Black, Black!' Rakhi stood up, slapped him hard and shouted, 'White! White! White!' There was a stunned silence, which was broken by the bus driver shouting, 'Bravo Rakhi!' All the children in the bus joined him with 'Bravo Rakhi, Bravo Rakhi!'

'I am very proud of you. Tell me, what would you like?' I said to Rakhi. She would like *'chorizo'* and Coca-Cola, was her prompt reply. *Chorizo* (a spicy pork sausage) was her favourite food and Coca-Cola was something I avoided buying, but which both of them loved. After celebrating the event, I asked Rakhi, 'What if the boys want to take their revenge?' 'I don't care,' was her response.

My respect for the school bus driver soared. By not keeping quiet and by getting all the children to support Rakhi, he had decisively kept the boys from taking their revenge. They could have otherwise cornered Rakhi in school and given her a thrashing.

When the time came to leave Mexico City at the end of my tenure, I went to the school to meet the bus driver. I was told that I might find him in the staff cafeteria. The cafeteria was large and full of people, benches, tables, and noise. I spotted him and as he saw and recognised me, he came to the corner where I was standing. I had gone well-prepared to express myself in Spanish and had taken a gift along with me. He greeted me, asked me to wait and disappeared.

After a while, he returned all breathless, with a bag full of chocolates and sweets, which he offered me with a broad grin and the words: *'Para las hijas'* (For the daughters). That smile is embedded in my memory. He is among those whom one does not meet again, but who remains with us somewhere in some corner of the heart.

Every place has its own language of behaviour. Spanish is the language of Mexico, but its language of behaviour is quite distinct from Spain. Politeness in Mexico is such that saying 'I don't know' is equated with rudeness. It was normal to be given totally misleading directions when one asked for help on the road. It was also not unusual for an invitation to lunch (dinner is not the preferred meal) to be gladly accepted, and for the invitee to either not turn up, or arrive when the last guest had already left. On one occasion, a couple brought along seven members of the family, without prior information, who were curious to have a taste of India. We were warned that guests were not expected to arrive at the given time. In fact, it would be embarrassing for our hosts if we were to arrive earlier than an hour or two after the given time.

One of the most appealing aspects of that culture is that women are equated with beauty. In short, by definition every woman is beautiful. Every woman is *'Que linda! Que bonita!'* (How attractive! How beautiful!). It was a Sunday afternoon. I had taken Rakhi and Meghna to the nearby park. They were excited to try their new skates. Mexico City has large sprawling parks with facilities for children and for skating. After strolling around, I sat down on a bench. A lively child was walking by, holding his grandfather's hand. When they approached me, the child stopped and said to his grandfather, 'Look how strange she is.' A sari was uncommon and the dot on my forehead must have added to the strangeness. The grandfather could not have known that I had a smattering of Spanish. He said to the child, 'You never say strange. You say how beautiful she is.'

Like other colonised countries, Mexico also carries the stamp of a lack of self-confidence. Our Embassy driver, Immanuel, was a good driver and a fine person also. It happened once that while driving, he averted a serious accident just in the nick of time. As he stepped suddenly on the brake to save a man who had appeared on the road right in front of the car, he let loose a stream of abuses, the last of which was: 'You Indo!' It was said with great anger. When we moved on, I could not restrain myself from asking him why he had called that man 'Indo'. To which, still quite agitated, he said, 'Because he is so foolish, such an idiot!' The irony was that Immanuel was himself an Indo.

This, of course, is not only peculiar to Mexico. In India, our love for fair skin and disdain for dark skin reflects the same mentality.

I have been an admirer of Gabriel García Márquez. I have read most of his novels and short stories, and some of them more than once. So when I was asked by the ICCR to extend an invitation to the writer for a lecture tour of India, I was only too glad to contact him. Márquez was born in Colombia. He started writing there, initially as a journalist. As the political situation in the country deteriorated, he shifted to Mexico City where he had been living for many years. He was a gregarious person. Despite my best efforts, however, I could not persuade him to accept our invitation. He said that he could not steal time from writing, which according to him would amount to theft. I was left to explain this in a long letter to the Government of India.

A few months later, I received in return an angry letter admonishing me in strong terms from Delhi. It appears that Márquez had accompanied his close friend Fidel Castro on the latter's visit to India to attend the summit of Non-Aligned countries. He had travelled on a Cuban passport along with Castro and his delegation. On the day of his departure from India, someone at the airport recognised Márquez. As a result, a storm broke out for me.

Like Pablo Neruda, Márquez was not comfortable with the poverty and the systems in place in India. Both writers were inclined towards socialist ideals.

Mexico City is a centre for creative artists. The visual arts and, especially, music and dancing, are woven into the life there. As I was relating, every Sunday, the 'Zócalo' or the main square in central Mexico City (from the word *zócalo*, meaning plinth) and smaller public squares all over the city would come to life with live orchestras. People would start dancing. Making a party, also called '*pachanga*', at the drop of a hat is second nature to Mexicans. This rhythm-based culture was struck by a natural disaster in September 1985.

I was getting my daughters ready for school in the morning when I heard the combined barking and howling of what seemed like all the dogs in the neighbourhood. This sound had hardly faded when I was knocked down. I tried to regain my balance, and fell again. Our cook Asha, who was preparing breakfast, began shrieking. Rakhi began to howl. Outside, there was something like the sound of thunder. The road had split into two. Mexico City had been struck by a massive earthquake which brought down 700 high-rise buildings like houses of cards in one stroke in the centre of town. Within moments, an estimated 10,000[1] people lay dead, and more than 35,000 were injured and buried under the rubble of their secure homes. All connections with the outside world were snapped. We wanted to inform our families that we were alive and could do so only two days later, after some connections had been restored. The large population of Mexico City which survived the disaster were either left homeless or did not have the courage to return to their unsafe homes. People occupied the vast areas of the city's parks. Successive tremors which followed the earthquake added to the fear of another disaster. Rakhi refused to come inside the house and decided to spend the night in the garden. I reasoned with her and tried to persuade her, but to no avail. She asked me, 'How do you know that there will not be another earthquake?' I had no answer. Finally, she agreed on the condition that all four of us would sleep together in one bed, to make sure that we would all die together. I agreed. Meghna found it very uncomfortable, so she shifted to her own bed.

While the city authorities took time to get their act together, the people of Mexico City reached out to help each other on a scale which has to be seen to be believed. They dug out people lying under the ruins of their houses with shovels and whatever implements they could assemble. Schools were turned into kitchens. The rich, poor, and middle class opened their doors to provide shelter and accommodate the homeless. The leisure and *pachanga*-loving people of the city had turned into a humanitarian army.

The previous year, in December 1984, I had gone to Delhi on home leave. The capital city had still not recovered from the assassination of Prime Minister Indira Gandhi (on 31 October 1984), and the widespread retaliatory killings of the Sikh community that followed. A very large-scale industrial disaster had also just struck Bhopal, the Bhopal gas tragedy of December 1984. The lack of concern for the sufferings of people due to man-made disasters, especially among the well-to-do Indians, was in stark contrast to what I witnessed in Mexico a year later. What could be the cause of such indifference to the helplessness of fellow citizens?

Could this indifference have puzzled writers like Pablo Neruda and García Márquez? Is it possible that it requires distance to be able to view the society of which we are a part?

Notes

1. *History*. 2009. '1985 Mexico City earthquake', 9 November. Available at https://www.history.com/topics/natural-disasters-and-environment/1985-mexico-city-earthquake (accessed June 2021).

7

Back to Vienna, 1986

I was delighted to receive the news that I had been posted once again to Vienna. The city was known to me. I was familiar with the narrow lanes of the 1st district, the home of Mozart and Beethoven. The language (German) was also close to my heart. The prospect of not having to learn a new language was especially welcome. Moreover, we had friends there, which made it feel like going home.

One of the first friends whom I contacted was Latika. About twenty years ago, she had come to Vienna from Bombay, as it was called then, on scholarship to learn music. She used to play the piano. I knew her when she was completing her course, and I was a probationer at the Embassy. I remember her first concert and visiting her at the music academy from time to time. We decided to meet in front of Stephansdom at 12 noon and settled in one of our known places, which was still there, for lunch. Latika told me that her Lebanese husband was a doctor. He was working in a small town not far from Vienna. She had two sons, and was so busy with her family responsibilities that coming to Vienna was a rare treat now. 'Are you teaching your sons to play the piano?' I asked her. She shook her head slowly to say 'no'.

'Surely they hear you play, and in time would want to learn,' I said reassuringly.

After a pause, Latika said very softly, 'I don't have a piano.'

Some weeks later, I was looking forward to meeting Latika at a piano concert by Horowitz, the famous pianist, whose visit was being awaited by the music audience of Vienna with enthusiasm and for which I had bought tickets, with some difficulty, for the two of us. On the day of the recital, she rang up to say that she would be unable to come. It was a memorable concert and I missed Latika.

In the fourteen years since I had last been there, some things had changed in Vienna. The U-Bahn (underground metro), the construction of which had just started when we left Vienna, was now a blessing for commuters. But many familiar shops had disappeared. The *schlachterei* (butcher's shop) where I used to buy meat had been replaced by a modern boutique. The *kohlmarkt* (coal market) had turned into a row of chic shops. 'Julius Meinl', the ambassador of Viennese coffeehouse culture, had been overtaken by 'Billa', a supermarket chain. The face of the 1st district was now glossy and custom-made for tourists. What I missed very much were the old-time eating places known as '*Gasthaus*', where one could eat off a fixed menu at a reasonable price and read all the newspapers of the day. What remained the same were the student artists playing music on the streets. On Sundays, apart from the violin, the horn, the accordion, and the flute, some enterprising musicians even played the piano now. A young Japanese pianist installed a grand piano at Stephansplatz one Sunday afternoon, and enthralled an audience among which was, along with us, our friend Kazimir Laski, who was for us a very special part of Vienna, as he was our oldest friend there. Vienna was more cosmopolitan now; a city which had once belonged to a greying generation had turned youthful.

To my utter delight, 'Heiner', the famous restaurant which served traditional dessert specialties handed down from the time of the Viennese royalty, was still there on Kärntner Strasse, the most famous shopping street in Central Vienna. In my enthusiasm to reveal my Vienna to my daughters, I took them to Heiner for a treat. Their reaction was lukewarm. In time, I learnt that we cannot share many of our treasured experiences with our children. We can also teach them very little of what we have learnt from our experiences. In short, every generation has to go to school, and learn according to its own inclinations.

During this phase in the late 1980s, there was growing unrest in Yugoslavia, one of Austria's close neighbours. After the death of President Tito (in 1980), who had held the reins of power very firmly in that country, there first began murmurs and then aggressive struggles between the provinces for separate statehood. President Tito had been, along with Nasser of Egypt and Nehru of India, one of the architects of the Non-Aligned Movement (NAM). This movement, which had been born with promise for the newly independent countries that had gained freedom from colonial stranglehold, had lost its momentum by then. The world was also looking different now. Although the Cold War had not ended, a wind of freedom of expression called *'perestroika'*[1] was blowing in the Soviet Union under the leadership of Mikhail Gorbachev.

In Vienna, one could often see photographs of the Soviet leader in shops in the 1st district. He was admired. His smiling face with the familiar birthmark on the forehead was a common sight. The struggles in Yugoslavia between the provinces began to turn bloody very soon.

Vienna was the seat of the International Atomic Energy Agency (IAEA) where India had been under pressure to sign the Treaty on the Non-Proliferation of Nuclear Weapons (NPT), something that had been resisted from the very beginning. In the meantime, other nations which had also resisted signing the treaty (like Argentina, Brazil, and South Africa) had changed their stance. The conferences of the IAEA were sometimes very lengthy. They would continue late into the night, like Hindustani classical music festivals. Delegates would go to the cafeteria to refresh themselves with a 'Kleiner Brauner' (or 'small brown', a kind of Viennese coffee that consists of a cup of espresso with a shot of milk on the side). The boredom of those unending conferences was broken by Nick, our Yugoslav colleague, who had a treasure trove of jokes and anecdotes to liven up our sagging spirits. East European jokes reflected the day-to-day hardships of the region. I remember one of his sparks: In a long queue (such queues were an abiding part of life in East European countries) where people had been standing for several hours to buy essential food supplies, a man lost his temper. In a fit of rage, he declared that he was quitting his place in the queue to go and kill the minister of supplies. He left. After sometime, he returned. 'Did you accomplish your objective?' people asked him in subdued voices. He replied, 'The queue there was much longer than the queue here.'

We were all disappointed when Nick was transferred back to Belgrade. I told his successor that we missed Nick and his lively jokes. To which he said to me, 'Those were the days of jokes. Now we have reality.' Indeed Yugoslavia, after much bloodshed, broke up into six new nations.

I remember very well the visit in 1989 of President Gorbachev to Berlin. In a press conference there, he was asked what he thought of the 'Berlin Wall', which was a symbol of the division of East and West Europe. Gorbachev's response was startling. He said that history was not static. Nothing was permanent. On hearing this, it seemed to me that in a few years, we might see the Wall coming down. Who could have imagined the speed with which the Wall came down and the geo-political map of Europe was redrawn? And that within three years, by 1991, the Soviet Union would split into fourteen new countries peacefully and without a drop of blood?

We witnessed the melting of large nations and the emergence of new ones like a drama being played before our eyes. Yet a discussion on 'nationalism' is not tolerated in 'nonviolent' India. It has been violently resisted by successive governments.

We continue to live by the principles of a colonial law which equates the nation with the government in power, and prohibits any criticism of the government. Criticism is treated as 'subversion'. It is the serious offence under which Gandhi, Nehru, and many freedom fighters during colonial rule were arrested and spent years in prison. The Sedition Act (Section 124A of the Indian Penal Code), a draconian law enacted in 1860 by the colonial State, should have been the first one to be rubbished and repealed in independent India. However, it has already survived and been made even stronger for seven violent decades after 1947, at great human cost, and there are no signs of it being revoked in the near future.

Very recently, in February 2017,[2] discussion on the concept of nationalism at one of Delhi University's colleges blew up into clashes between the organisers and participants of the seminar, and the ABVP (Akhil Bharatiya Vidyarthi Parishad), a Right-wing student front, which would not allow it because it would be, by their definition, an 'anti-national' act to discuss nationalism.

During my second posting in Vienna, we lived in a 100-year-old apartment on Burgring, right in front of the Burggarten Park, next to the Hofburg Palace. Our windows opened to a view of Mozart's statue which stands in the park in green surroundings, amid flowers during summer. The picture in autumn is equally, if not even more, attractive, as the park is transformed into a yellow-and-golden cover of tree leaves. In Vienna's winter, the Burggarten and the statue are covered with a thick blanket of snow. This is one of the most frequented sites for tourists visiting the city. It was very convenient for us to have a tram stop right below the apartment.

Vienna's winters can be quite harsh, especially when the cold winds from the east penetrate right to the bones. On one such winter evening, when returning from office, I saw that the *Sardar ji* (a title used to refer to Sikh men) who used to sell newspapers at the tram stop was not wearing anything warm. I brought down one of my husband's coats and gave it to him to wear. After that, we greeted each other occasionally.

Our time in Vienna was approaching its end. I was going to go back to India. One morning, I received a call from the police headquarters. I was asked if I knew a person by the name of Harpreet Singh. It sounded like a Punjabi name, but I could not recall or connect it to anybody I knew. I asked in what context I was being questioned. The police clarified that they had in their custody an Indian by this name, who had said that he wanted to speak to me and that I knew him. Over the telephone, he said to me, 'Madam *ji*, I am Harpreet Singh. You remember you gave me a coat? The police arrested me, along with other men with whom I share a roof at night, on charges of drug trafficking. But you know that I sell newspapers. Please tell them.'

With my intervention, Harpreet Singh was released. He looked much thinner, and quite down and out. I gave him some money to start life again. A few days later, he turned up at the Embassy to see me again, looking clean and smiling. He said that he was a carpenter by profession, and wanted to make a piece of furniture for me. He could make me a cupboard, a dressing table, or just anything that I would like. I told him that I was not in need of any furniture, and would soon be leaving for India. He was disappointed.

Three years later, I was posted to Hamburg as Consul General. I had barely settled there when my secretary told me that there was somebody from Vienna who was calling me persistently, someone by the name of Harpreet Singh, who said that I knew him very well. I could not recall the name, but took the call.

'I am Harpreet Singh, Madam *ji*. Don't you remember, you gave me a coat?'

'Yes, how are you, Harpreet Singh? How did you know that I am in Hamburg?' I asked him. I was quite puzzled.

'I have been asking the Embassy about you, and they told me that you are now posted in Hamburg. They gave me your telephone number. Now my family, wife and children, have also joined me. We are well settled here. Please tell me what I can make for you and bring to Hamburg. Hamburg is not too far from Vienna, Madam *ji*, I will bring it,' he said.

Actually, for me Vienna has never been too far. Amit was a visiting professor in Linz and then in Vienna. His academic ties and collaborations deepened with time and became stronger. He often visited Vienna. I have seldom missed a chance to accompany him to my *lieblingsstadt* (favourite city), Vienna.

Notes

1. *Perestroika* was a liberal movement to restructure Soviet economic and political policy in the mid-1980s.

2. On 21 and 22 February 2017, a two-day seminar titled 'Cultures of Protest—Unveiling the State: Regions in Conflict', organised by the English department and the literary society of Delhi University's Ramjas

College, led to violent protests over the participation of JNU (Jawaharlal Nehru University) student leaders. The ABVP, a Right-wing student front, declared the student leaders 'anti-nationals', locked down the college seminar room, and pelted stones in protest, thereby forcing the college authorities to rescind the invitation. When a section of teachers, students, and members of the AISA (All India Students' Association) attempted to peacefully march to the local police station, they were attacked by the ABVP. Several eminent professors, journalists, and students were injured.

See *India Times*. 2017. 'Here's What Happened At Ramjas College That Led To The Clashes Between ABVP, AISA And Delhi Police', 24 February. Available at https://www.indiatimes.com/news/here-s-what-happened-at-ramjas-college-that-led-to-the-clashes-between-abvp-aisa-and-delhi-police-272175.html (accessed January 2021).

Also, see *The Hindu*. 2017. 'Clashes at Ramjas College in Delhi over cancellation of invite to Umar Khalid', 22 February. Available at https://www.thehindu.com/news/cities/Delhi/clash-between-du-students-and-abvp-members/article17346639.ece (accessed January 2021).

8

Hamburg, 1992

One of the richest cities of Europe, situated on the Elbe River a short distance from the sea, Hamburg belongs to the traditionally trade-dominated centres historically known as the Hanseatic League.[1] These cities had the distinction of being governed by traders, not by princes. Their city centres were built around the dominant position of the trading house, in front of which stood the administration and government. The church stood a short distance away in the third place. Others among the Hanseatic states were Bremen, Rostock, and the principal city of the *hansa*, the beautiful town of Lübeck. I was posted as Consul General to Hamburg in 1992. My responsibilities extended to include all these towns and the whole of North Germany, including Schleswig-Holstein. Amit was invited to be visiting professor at the University of Bremen, which was a commutable distance away. Later, he was a fellow at the Centre of Advanced Studies in Berlin, still not too far from Hamburg.

Like most German cities, Hamburg is very efficiently administered. Its pulse, however, lies in its trading activities, and the place of the church in the life of its people has been diminishing. There was a time when people shared their problems with the parish priest and sought his advice. That position has long been taken over by psychiatrists, who charge hefty sums for expensive advice. The role of the church is now becoming increasingly restricted to providing funeral services. I remember a remark made by my friend Margaret Wenz when I asked her why she continued to pay church tax when she was not religious, and did not ever attend Sunday church. 'I will need the church for my burial,' she had said.

The situation in India is quite the opposite. Our godmen do not only offer advice, but they also provide a network of security and society to lonely individuals. Their business is thriving, extending beyond their living space into TV channels and even abroad. The more popular amongst them are multi-millionaires with access to the highest political ranks.

On my arrival as Consul General of India, I was welcomed by the tea traders in Hamburg and their associations with large receptions and long speeches. Many of the importers of Indian tea had been in the trade for a long time, some for more than two generations. Hamburg is the port of the largest tea imports from India in Europe. The tea traders have elegant shops with fancy prices. I was appalled to learn that the Government of India was giving them US$ 1 million every year, in the interest of 'export promotion'. My opinion that this contribution from a poor country to one of the wealthiest trading associations in the world made little sense and advice to have it discontinued fell on deaf ears. By now, I was no longer a beginner and had learnt the limitations of my profession, so I was not altogether surprised to not receive so much as an acknowledgement of my letter from the Commerce Ministry in Delhi.

A regular and invariable refrain at all gatherings organised by the tea traders was that they were facing a big problem: the market for Darjeeling tea had been stolen from them. A certain Professor Faltin in Berlin was, through his 'nefarious activities', causing them heavy losses. This aroused my curiosity. I was driving to Dresden for a conference and decided to meet the professor on my way in Berlin. He gave me an appointment and also agreed to have lunch with me.

This was my first long journey through united Germany. East and West had come together in 1990, but the East side still looked very different and less prosperous. There was a lot of building activity on roads, and even more prominent was the ongoing activity of placing new roofs on house tops. There were visible signs of unemployment. Unemployed youth stood in groups in the centre of towns.

Professor Faltin's place was very close to the house of Günter Grass, the famous German writer. The professor taught economics at the university, but this place where I was to meet him was where his project was located. He asked me if I was interested in seeing his project, which he had launched along with his students as part of their course. He showed me around three to four rooms where his students collected mail and post from buyers of Darjeeling tea from all over the country, and then packed and posted the product directly to them. Not a penny had been spent in setting up shop, and even more interestingly, nothing was spent on advertisement. I told him that his competitors in Hamburg and Bremen were losing their sleep after having lost their market to him. He laughed and explained that the tea traders would mix one part of Darjeeling tea with nine parts of Assam tea, and then pass it off as Darjeeling tea, which they would sell at exorbitant prices. He, on the other hand, was selling pure Darjeeling tea. The consumer was buying genuine quality tea for a fair price. There was no need for advertisement. People learnt about it through word of mouth. In course of time, I met many people who were buying tea by post from Berlin.

That afternoon, we walked to a nearby restaurant for lunch. I found Professor Faltin a soft-spoken and modest person. The place he had chosen for lunch was unpretentious. As we sat down, he asked me how I had come to learn about him. 'I was told about you by your enemies, who want to kill you,' I told him. He laughed heartily at my reply. After this meeting, I seldom missed a chance to meet the professor when I was in Berlin. The last time we met, he was working on designing a new type of brick. He presented to me a small sample of the brick in white porcelain, which is among my carefully-kept precious objects.

This was a phase in Germany when unemployment was high and the presence of foreigners, especially Turks, was being resented. The general complaint was that foreigners made no effort to join the 'mainstream'. To my Indian ears, this sounded very familiar. The majority communities in all democracies have the same complaint. Why don't the minority communities eat what we like? Why don't they dress and speak as we do? The list is unending.

To counter this prejudiced behaviour, a movement was launched by some liberal and open-minded people. They went to schools, colleges, institutions, and door-to-door, explaining the dangers of treating minorities as unwanted people. Finally, a massive march was organised around the Alster Lake in the centre of Hamburg to show solidarity towards minorities and foreigners and point out that they are also human. I could not resist joining this march, which included men, women, very old people, and children in such large numbers as one is not used to seeing in Europe. As the evening grew darker, candles in the hands of the marchers illuminated the town and the lake, reminding me of Diwali back home. A few days later, in another part of town through which I was passing, my attention was caught by the title of an exhibition, which read something like this: 'Somewhere or the other, each one of us is a minority.'

Even in our own country, we can become a minority. A Punjabi in Chennai, a Bengali in Punjab, a Tamilian in Assam—they are minorities in their own country. If we are willing to understand this reality, then we could avoid being either the oppressors or the oppressed, depending on where we are. In Germany, the efficient killing of six million Jews in specially constructed gas chambers during Hitler's regime had tarnished the image of the country as a civilised nation. The Jews, too, had been a minority community. As I write these lines, a storm has broken out in America among people of Indian origin because an Indian has been shot dead in a bar in Kansas in a racially motivated murder.[2] The seeds of the targeting of minorities, to a large extent, lie within the idea of democracy itself, which is: rule by the majority, which turns into rule for the majority. Democratic countries have yet to evolve safeguards to protect minorities from majority oppression.

Indians settled in America, who had felt quite comfortable till very recently, and who had been generally unconcerned about the plight of 'others' like African-Americans, suddenly found themselves in the company of the latter, being persecuted and discriminated against.

To return to the efforts to improve majority–minority relations in Hamburg in 1992, some intellectuals of Hamburg had organised a lecture by a highly respected Rabbi from Israel in a prestigious hall in the city centre. The eloquent speaker traced the history of the oppression of Jews that stretched over 2,000 years. Keeping in mind the undercurrent of guilt in a German audience, he had steered clear of mentioning the fate of the Jews in Germany's recent history. His point was that the State of Israel still faced hostility, bordering on oppression, from its neighbours. At the end of his speech, he offered to answer questions from the audience. There was an uncomfortable silence till I decided to ask a question which had bothered me. Hitler's large-scale killing of Jews had not happened overnight. It was preceded by the passing of many laws which discriminated against the Jews. First, rules were made so they could not continue their studies, then they could not keep to their chosen professions, next they could not keep their jobs, and step by step, in this manner, they were edged out. They had to give up their professions, then their properties, till finally, they had nothing left to give up except their lives. Those Jews who had read the writing on the wall left Germany. Among them were well-known intellectuals like Albert Einstein and Sigmund Freud, as well as leading bankers. The Jewish community of Europe lacked neither money nor intellectuals, scientists, and professionals; why then did it not organise itself to resist and protest the methodical annihilation of the community?

The distinguished Rabbi waited and then said to the large gathering, 'Our children ask us this very question. We have no answer.'

Every minority community has to face this question. Since somewhere or the other we are all a minority, the question is relevant to all of us. To seek protection is one thing; to organise protest is another. Without organising protest, the chances of getting protection are dim. The Dalit community in India was given some protection by the Constitution of the country, but even after seven decades of independence, their plight is deplorable. Of late, a slight wind of change has been visible in better organisation and bolder forms of protest. Hopefully, this wind will gather force.

Bremen, which is another Hanseatic city, is situated relatively close to Hamburg. I was approached by the authorities to put up an exhibition on India in one of the old and historical warehouses of the town. The idea appealed to me. With the help of the then Director of the National Crafts Museum and Hastkala Academy in Delhi, Jyotendra Jain, whom I had come to know during my first posting in Vienna many years ago, a somewhat different kind of exposition was worked out, at the heart of which was a display by the weavers (of silk cloth) of Benares on their traditional looms, which involved the weaving of intricate designs in colourful silk threads mixed with gold and silver threads. What added charm to the display was the fact that people could buy what they saw being woven, and the weavers were happy to sell their craft to growing numbers of buyers who started arriving from far-off towns. The second big attraction was an exhibition of Indian cartoons and an interaction with our famous cartoonist, R. K. Laxman. He had accepted my invitation and had come with his wife, along with some exceptionally good samples of his perceptive sketches. I recall the delightful walk we had along the narrow lanes of the old town of Bremen. Laxman would find something special and call his wife, Kamala, to draw her attention to it. He was almost childlike in his unfailing enthusiasm. He was, of course, a very good talker. At a dinner at my house and after a little whiskey (which was his favourite drink), he had us in splits of laughter as he narrated some of his experiences with the important people of Mumbai, who did not always take well to his jokes. About Rajiv Gandhi, he said that the Prime Minister had the habit of dismissing any complaint with the words: 'Will look into the matter.' On one occasion when they met, Rajiv Gandhi complained to Laxman that he always made him appear fat in his cartoons. To which Laxman said: 'Will look into the matter, Sir.'

During the exhibition, I was reminded of the accuracy of Professor Faltin's perceptive comment that advertisement was unnecessary where value was evident. It seemed to me that the breeze from Bremen and word of mouth were sufficient to draw large numbers of people to the exhibition. One of the frequent visitors to the long exhibition was Herr Riezig. He was an elderly gentleman familiar with India, having visited the country several times over many years, from the mountains in the north to the sea coasts of the east and west. Once, sitting over a glass of wine, he related some of his experiences. I found his observations quite perceptive. At one point, I asked him what he found special in the behavioural language of Indians. 'You might be disappointed,' he said. 'That is immaterial,' I replied, and coaxed him to share his views with me. These, he pointed out, were his observations about the general behaviour of people in India: 'There is a subservient attitude towards those in authority,' he said. People bow down to those in authority, and are harsh towards those below them. In short—and these are my words, not his—lick the boots of those above you, and kick those below you.

He then asked me about my impression of German behaviour. From my limited experience, I had gathered the impression that generally, people were very conscious of their rights and in upholding established rules and regulations. They did not hesitate to ensure that others did the same. I recalled an instance. It was a cold and stormy night after heavy snowfall. We were fast asleep when the doorbell rang around 2 AM. Amit opened the door and was taken aback to see a police officer, along with our landlord. They said that they had received information that a fire had broken out in our house. Starting with the kitchen, they checked every corner of the house. There was no trace of a fire. What they discovered was that on the terrace, a light bulb had not been switched off. Till late in the evening, Rakhi and Meghna had been playing with snow on the terrace. The general conclusion was that someone had mistaken the light of the bulb in the raging snowstorm for fire. What I found strange was the fact that someone in the neighbourhood had been observing with a telescope, from a long distance, what was taking place during a snowstorm on our terrace, because the distance between houses was considerable.

On another occasion on a Sunday afternoon in summer, I went to my favourite ice cream shop. When I returned to the car with several packets of ice cream in my arms, I was met by three concerned citizens. Two of them were young boys, about twelve or fourteen years old. The third was a very well-groomed young lady in a Jaguar. All three handed over to me the number of a car, which they said had bumped into mine. The elderly lady who had accidentally hit my car had not done what is normally done, that is, leave her name and insurance particulars on my windscreen. She had just driven off! They said that they would accompany me to the police station to register a case against the offender. I looked at the damage done to my car. It was a small scratch. It did not cause me any distress. But it was difficult for me to refuse the solidarity extended by the three conscientious citizens. My real dilemma was that the ice cream was in danger of melting into a river.

In some situations, Germans turn into self-made policemen. Herr Riezig summed it up by saying that although emotions, pain, and laughter are common to all, spoken and behavioural languages distinguish one group of people from another.

As Consul General in Hamburg, my area of responsibility extended to Schleswig-Holstein. This is also called the Switzerland of Germany. It is indeed a very attractive area, bordering on Denmark. For several centuries, it was a bone of serious contention between Germany and Denmark. Both countries claimed it as rightfully theirs. Somewhat resembling the Kashmir dispute in our part of the world, many skirmishes and wars were fought and much blood was shed over the question of possession of Schleswig-Holstein. The issue was finally resolved, but only after both Denmark and democratic post-war Germany were bound in a common strategic bond, the Bonn–Copenhagen Declarations[3] of 1955, which are today considered a model for dealing with minority issues in Europe, with the principles of tolerance, liberality, and reciprocity finding their reflection in both countries' policies. Visiting this beautiful, undulating, green, and prosperous land always gave me the hope that some seemingly hopeless disputes between nations can be resolved in the least expected of ways.

Notes

1. During the Late Middle Ages, the Hanseatic League (from Old High German *'Hansa'*, meaning guild) was a commercial and defensive confederation of merchant guilds and market towns in Northwestern and Central Europe. Growing from a few North German towns in the late 1100s, the League came to dominate Baltic maritime trade for three centuries along the coasts of Northern Europe and diminished slowly after 1450.

2. On 22 February 2017, at a suburban Kansas City bar, two Indian men became the victims of a hate crime. Srinivas Kuchibhotla was killed while his co-worker, Alok Madasani, was wounded. See *The New York Times*. 2017. 'Hate Crime Is Feared as 2 Indian Engineers Are Shot in Kansas', 24 February. Available at https://www.nytimes.com/2017/02/24/world/asia/kansas-attack-possible-hate-crime-srinivas-kuchibhotla.html (accessed January 2021).

3. *Federal Foreign Office*. 2015. '60 years since the signing of the Bonn-Copenhagen Declarations: the German-Danish friendship in action', 30 March. Available at https://www.auswaertiges-amt.de/en/aussenpolitik/laenderinformationen/daenemark-node/150326-steinmeier-lidegaard-albig/270486 (accessed January 2021).

9

Minsk and Lithuania, 1996

I was disappointed when I was posted as Ambassador to Minsk, Belarus. The idea of learning Russian was daunting. Minsk, like Hanoi in 1975, was a hardship posting, designated as a 'C*' posting (where living conditions are hard) in the Ministry. Normally, such postings are restricted to a term of two years. My tenure in Minsk was extended to four years, which speaks rather poorly of my popularity with the administration in Delhi. Amit, Rakhi, and Meghna could join me in Minsk only during their vacations. Along with Minsk, I was also accredited as Ambassador to Vilnius, Lithuania.

Belarus was emerging as a new nation after the recent breakup of the Soviet Union. Like other breakaway nations, they were trying to find their feet. Belarus was special. A part of the Soviet Union bordering Poland, Belarus had historically prided itself for having defended Russia throughout its history. It was the part of the Soviet Union where the defence industry was located, and its large professional class had the highest standard of living during Soviet times. In a referendum held in March 1991 before the breakup of the Soviet Union, 83 per cent of the people of Belarus had voted in favour of preserving the Soviet Union. It was then President Yeltsin's (the first President of Russia, 1991–99) vulnerability to American and NATO (North Atlantic Treaty Organization) pressure that forced Belarus into becoming a separate nation, despite the overwhelming desire of the people to remain a part of Russia. The loud voices of Western democracy turn very undemocratic when it comes to their perception of what constitutes their own 'strategic interest'. I cannot think of another such example in the creation of nations. What is more, the reins of power in Minsk were soon grabbed by a young communist party leader, Alexander Lukashenko, who has since then held onto them firmly and continues to dominate the political scene. Hailed as Europe's last dictator, Lukashenko has been the first and only President of Belarus since the office was established in 1994. In his regime, any dissenting voice has been silenced even before it had had a chance to be heard. No opposition has been allowed to emerge. Any signs of it are nipped in the bud. However, over the last one year, following the 2020 presidential elections, a strong people's movement has taken to the streets in protest against the rigging of elections in favour of Lukashenko.[1]

Although freedom of expression has not been allowed throughout Lukashenko's reign, he has kept in check dissatisfaction of the type that was rampant in neighbouring Ukraine and Russia, where the end of the socialist system created extreme hardship for a people used to being looked after from cradle to grave. In Belarus, the socialist system remained unchanged under Lukashenko. Belarusians were relieved. Free accommodation, free hot water provided by the municipalities, and free cooking gas, along with employment and healthcare altogether provided ample compensation to people, who watched their relatives in Russia and Ukraine being left to fend for themselves, bereft of the economic security which they had been used to for seven decades.

The scene in the neighbouring Baltic State of Lithuania was mixed. The end of Russian domination was welcomed. Lithuania had once been a part of Germany and between 1941–44, the Germans had been at first welcomed as liberators from the repressive Soviet regime, but soon Lithuanian attitudes towards the Germans had changed into passive resistance. Independent Lithuania now aspired to be part of West Europe. It looked to the West to sort out its economic problems. During this period, it was interesting to watch the evolution of democracy in Lithuania. Almost all the fourteen nations which had emerged from the breakup of the Soviet Union had opted for a presidential form of government. The result, almost in every capital, was confrontation between the President and the

Parliament. The most striking was the Russian constitutional crisis of 1993, marked by the firing on the Parliament in Moscow by army tanks on President Boris Yeltsin's orders (known as the October coup). At the climax of the crisis, Russia was thought to be on the brink of civil war. Such instability was deftly averted in Vilnius by President Brazauskas's intrinsic commitment to democracy. He did not allow a confrontation to happen in those early days.

The geographical distance between Minsk and Vilnius was just a two-hour drive by car. However, the difference in the directions of nation-building taken by the two neighbours grew rapidly. I had arrived at a crucial time in the breaking and making of history in East Europe.

The residences of ambassadors in Minsk were located in the vast area of President Lukashenko's official estate, which included lakes and forested tracts. The boundary between the residences of President Lukashenko and the Indian Ambassador was formed by a row of birch trees and many flowering shrubs. Through these bushes and trees, the President's favourite dog often used to visit us. He was usually followed and gently taken away by security guards. This seemed to me to be a prized game which the esteemed dog liked to play. Perhaps he was also attracted by the fragrance of apples, pears, blackberries, and plums in our garden.

Mariana, my young maid and cook, kept herself very busy. When I asked her what she was busy with, her invariable reply was, 'I am preparing for winter'. On a Sunday in late autumn, I saw in the kitchen rows of large glass jars of pickled vegetables and fruit jams, which she had made from the crops collected in the garden. Autumn is a beautiful season, especially when the birch trees turn yellow and golden. There is a Russian saying to the effect that women, like the season of autumn, are the most beautiful in the autumn of their lives.

As the trees and bushes shed their leaves, Mariana asked me one day to follow her to the terrace. There, she pointed to the President's house. Deprived of the cover of foliage, which had provided it graceful privacy, the President's house stood openly visible. Mariana looked very pleased.

I was a little perplexed that everyone called her Marina, while I was the only one who called her Mariana. Could it be that I was so used to the name Mariana in Mexico, and she was too polite to correct me? When I asked her if I should correct myself, she was thoughtfully silent. Finally, she made it clear that she wanted me to continue calling her Mariana. The secret of this perplexity took a long time to unravel. Russian television used to show a Mexican serial which was thunderingly popular, the name of the very popular heroine of which was Mariana.

I recall that on my return from Vilnius after presenting my credentials to President Brazauskas, Mariana asked me how I found Vilnius. Did I like it? She was eager to know. Not realising how loaded that question was, I answered, 'It's a very charming place.' To this, she said gravely, 'You know that during the war, Lithuanian people supported Hitler?' She had caught me off guard. The devastation of World War II, which took the lives of an estimated twenty-six[2] million Russians, has survived in the memory of more than three generations. The memorial to the dead Russian soldiers is located in Khatyn, a vast barren area, not far from Minsk. There is no big monument built in the usual Soviet style. There are small grave-like structures, although these are not graves, scattered as far as the eye can see. A bell rings every two minutes, breaking the bleak silence in memory of a soldier, of a life lost. Hitler was defeated by the Soviet Union at a very heavy price.

During my first year in Minsk, an important delegation of Indian scientists came from the Defence Research and Development Organisation (DRDO). The delegation was led by the then chief of DRDO, A. P. J. Abdul Kalam, who later became the eleventh President of India (2002–07). I was appalled to see Dr Kalam arrive on a cold January morning, wearing a thin jacket which might be just right for Delhi winters. The idea of wearing one of Amit's warm jackets was laughed away by him, 'Ambassador, you think I will fall ill and become a burden on you. Don't worry, I will be fine.' In that bitter cold, he went for long walks in the morning, deep in thought, as though he were walking in Delhi in November. He was a vegetarian. Sushma, my cook, was delighted at his appreciation of the *idli* and *sambar* (South Indian cuisine) that she made. He took no alcohol, and made his Russian hosts very nervous with his eating habits. The Belarusian government hosted a large banquet for him. The chief of protocol called on me to discuss, very seriously, what should be prepared for the chief guest. That Dr Kalam would like boiled rice and curd, which is called *kefir*[3] there, and would stick to drinking juice and water was unthinkable and very contrary to Russian hospitality, a hospitality unmatched anywhere else that I have been to in my many travels. The only person not surprised was Professor Oleg Vladislavovich Roman, who was an old friend of Dr Kalam and had spent a lot of time with him on building the infrastructure for developing missile technology in India. From Soviet times, the two had been collaborating to lay the groundwork for missile technology, which is a very big success story in India today. Over time, I came to know Professor Roman and his family better. Both Professor Roman and I shared an interest in and love for music.

At my request, a special ballet performance was organised for Dr Kalam and his team. That morning, I had handed over to Dr Kalam his honorarium and travel allowances in an envelope. He had slipped it into his pocket without opening it. At the end of a magnificent performance, the audience gave a standing ovation, and Dr Kalam took out the unopened envelope from his pocket and handing it over to me, whispered, 'Ambassador, please hand this to the artists as a gesture of our appreciation.'

Collaboration between DRDO and its Belarusian counterpart led to frequent visits. On one such visit by DRDO scientists to Minsk, after dinner at my residence, there was an animated discussion, during which one of the Indian scientists asked, 'Why did Central Europe, which had been home to and the nurturer of the best mathematicians and scientists before World War II, lose that position after the war?' I saw that Professor Roman was lost in thought and remained silent, so I shared my view on the question. A very large number of intellectuals, mathematicians, and scientists in Europe had been Jews. Hitler's war on Jews and his 'final solution' to eliminate them had led to a large-scale emigration of the community. Among those who fled were people like Albert Einstein and Ludwig Wittgenstein. Those who did not migrate were sent to concentration camps fitted with gas chambers. The result was that Europe after the war had turned into a desert, bereft of intellectuals and scientists among them.

I noticed that Professor Roman looked very serious and his eyes were fixed on me; I wondered why. The conversation moved on. Professor Roman was the last of my guests to leave. He held my hand, bent and kissed it. When he raised his head, I thought I saw tears in his eyes.

By profession, Professor Roman's daughter, Olga, was a doctor. She was also a talented cook. The dinner table in Professor Roman's house was testimony to her culinary skills. One Sunday, in summer, at my request she taught me how to bake bread filled with cabbage. After that, she took me to discover parts of the city which were unknown to me. The old town of Minsk is a small area occupied by twelve rickety old wooden houses which had survived the bombing by the German army. The rest of the town was reduced to rubble. Minsk was a special target for Hitler for two reasons: One, because it provided the strongest resistance to the German army on its way to Moscow, and two, because Jews formed a very large proportion of its population. As we walked past the remains of Minsk's history, Olga pointed to the north and said, 'This was where the Jews lived. My grandmother's house was there.'

'Where was she during the war?' I asked her.

'She fled with her son to Vladivostok. They lived in poverty there and returned only after the war.'

Although the ideology of the Soviet Union was against racial discrimination, centuries of social prejudice ran too deep to be uprooted. It still survives. The prejudice against Jews, better known as anti-Semitism, is spread over Europe with deep roots in Poland, Belarus, and also Lithuania. The most attractive city centre of Vilnius, which resembles Italian towns, was to a large extent owned by Jews. The high-class Esterházy Jews[4] from this region formed the creators and ruling elite of Israel. Israeli Prime Minister Golda

Meier was from Belarus, and so was Shimon Peres, former president and prime minister of Israel.

I used to visit Vilnius quite frequently. The speed with which this run-down Soviet town was turning into a lively European face was quite amazing. Unlike in Minsk, rapidly growing private ownership was giving Vilnius a face lift. It amazed me that the first private shops to open were perfumeries. It seemed that cosmetics were the top priority of people here. Small and charming hotels followed. Music and theatre were as much a part of life in Vilnius as in Belarus, although the standard of music and ballet in Belarus was way above that of Vilnius; it even surpassed that of Petersburg, Russia. The 'Lithuanian' language, very strangely, has a strong connection with India. The spoken language, Lithuanian, has 1,200 words of Sanskrit in common use. There is an old department of Sanskrit at the university in Vilnius. I saw a lively theatre presentation of Kalidasa's *Abhigyan Shakuntalam*. The music of that drama left me curious because it had a strong touch of Hindustani classical music. I sought out the music director and found, to my utter amazement, that he had been a student of Pandit Pran Nath. Pran Nath used to head the department of Hindustani classical music at Delhi University in the 1960s; he had also been my teacher.

Quite unexpectedly, at an art exhibition in Vilnius, I came face to face with the thirteenth-century monument of Hauz Khas in Delhi. The artist was Filomina, who had travelled many times to India. Her sketches seemed alive and captured the ambience very skilfully. Two of her sketches are among my valued possessions. As I write these lines, the mosque in Mandu,[5] Madhya Pradesh, sketched by Filomina, faces me on the wall before me. She was a sensitive artist and fluent in many languages. I was taken aback when, in the course of a conversation, she casually declared, 'I hate the Russians, but I hate the Jews even more.' It seems to me that social prejudices are a way of finding a scapegoat for deprivations. It is a need of the prejudiced mind.

On a beautiful autumn evening, I was to meet Filomina at her favourite coffee shop. I found her looking pale and sad.

'Is something the matter?' I asked her.

She sighed deeply and said, 'I have been through a trauma.'

'What happened?' I enquired.

'My son got married,' she replied sadly.

'I remember you telling me that he was getting married to the lovely daughter of the most respected and famous surgeon of your country.'

'Yes. My son is no longer mine,' she said sadly.

In Lithuania, they say that every woman thinks that her husband is stupid, that her son is extraordinary, and that she never has enough clothes.

In Minsk, the long, severe winter months are balanced by ballet and musical performances of very high calibre. I have come to the conclusion that the best of music and literature was born in Europe during the long cold winters. I was leaving for a music concert on an evening of heavy snowfall when the telephone rang. It was Karim Ahmed on the line. Ahmed was heading a World Bank institution in Minsk, and said that he was speaking from the railway station, where he had found a young Indian man lying semi-conscious in the snow. He wanted to know if he could bring the destitute Indian to the Embassy in his car.

Had Karim not found Raju Marwari that evening and brought him to the Embassy, that young man would not have survived under the heavy snowfall that night. He had on him only a thin shirt. He had not eaten in days and had been beaten, robbed of his jacket and what little money he had by the police, which in no country is kind to the illegal immigrant. After medical treatment and many days of care supervised by Jogendra Bhagat, the consular assistant at the Embassy, who was an exceptionally kind person, Raju was able to speak and finally stand on his feet. Psychologically and physically, he was far from normal, even when he was able to walk and talk coherently.

Raju told Bhagat that he came from a large family in Ludhiana, Punjab. His parents had raised a large sum of Rs 3,00,000 with much difficulty to finance his ambition to reach Germany with the aid of an 'agent', and make a comfortable living there. The agent, for that hefty price, had procured a passport for him and promised to fly him from Delhi to Frankfurt. Along with other young men, Raju was not taken to Frankfurt but to Moscow, and from there transported stealthily by train to somewhere near Minsk. The passports of the young men were taken by the agent. At night, they were dumped close to a forest. While getting off the train, Raju fell and was injured. He lost contact with the group. He finally reached Minsk, was caught by the police, and was beaten and robbed of the little that he had; and then he made it to the railway station, where Karim Ahmed found him. He related this to Bhagat, whom he had begun to trust. But Bhagat's advice to him to return to Punjab was difficult for him to accept. Getting a visa for Poland and for Germany (Poland was the country of transit to reach Germany) was out of the question, and letting agents transport him illegally was dangerous. There was not much choice. Raju was able to speak to his father over the telephone, and his father was of the view that he had to give reaching Germany a good try. After all, they had collected with so much difficulty the money which had been paid to the agent. Finally, I had to tell his father that Raju was not physically fit to run the risk of illegally travelling to Poland and Germany. Did the father want to see his son alive? The father was persuaded. We arranged for Raju to travel to Moscow, and to be helped by the Indian Embassy there to board an Air India flight to Delhi, from where Raju's brother would take him home to Ludhiana.

On the afternoon that Raju left, the police telephoned us to say that about sixty illegal Indian immigrants had been caught in the nearby forest. They were in police custody. Bhagat went to the police station, and I spoke to the Home Minister of Belarus. With his intervention, the lost, hungry, and desperate young men were released. It turned out that about ten of them were Pakistani. They were very grateful for our help. Since there was no Pakistani Embassy in Belarus, I advised them to contact their Embassy in Moscow. Bhagat took charge of finding accommodation and providing food for them.

The horror stories of how these men were packed in a container were recorded by Bhagat. The container had no provision for air. The men could hardly breathe. It was driven at a very high speed and it overturned. As luck would have it, the door flung open and the men were thrown out. Many of them had sustained injuries. One lost half his teeth in the accident. Bhagat's small video camera recorded the misadventures of these rather innocent young men who had sold land belonging to their fathers to collect the fee charged by the agents. The land mafia and the agents had together made good money on these transactions. The sellers were the losers.

The arrest of illegal Indians turned into an uninterrupted stream. Before we could persuade one lot to return home, the arrest of another group was reported. Persuading the young men to return to Punjab was a difficult task. Not only had their fathers sold land and their mothers' ornaments, but their wives also had dreams of a better life. One of them told us frankly, 'We are not trapped by the agents. We willingly go to them. We also want a TV, a TV antenna on our house, a small Maruti car, and a higher standard of living like those families whose relatives are in America and Germany, from where they send them money.'

It was difficult, they said, for them to return. They would look like cowards. They had lost not just money, but their face. Bhagat was able to convince them that turning back when one comes to a dead end is not an act of cowardice. It is an act of courage. I remember telling them that they were all young and strong; they could give the agents a beating if they wanted. What was there to be afraid of?

More than 300 illegal immigrants returned to India. One of them rang us up to say that he had given a thrashing to his agent, and got back from him the money that he had paid him.

Bhagat's video clips gradually took the form of a documentary film called *Road to Germany* (1997). The film was shown on some channels in India. In those days, there were only a few channels. Doordarshan showed parts of it in a weekly programme on investigative journalism, called 'Aankhon Dekhi'. The issue of the plight of illegal immigrants at the hands of agents drew a lot of attention in Punjab. The stories of the young men who were returning to Punjab were given prominence in Punjabi newspapers. *The Times of India* carried an editorial, and *The Indian Express* provided extensive coverage. *Road to Germany* also caught the attention of the German press.

One of the most difficult things we had to face were the threatening calls which Bhagat started to receive from the mafia (of immigration rackets that illegally transported people from India, Pakistan, and Bangladesh to Europe). His children had to stop going to school and his wife was confined to the house at one point in time. By the time Bhagat was posted back to India, the route for illegal immigration through Belarus and Poland to Germany had changed.

Bhagat was succeeded at the Embassy by V. Radha, another very fine consular officer. I was lucky to have Radha as my assistant not only in Minsk, but also later in Lisbon. Officers like Bhagat and Radha are an asset wherever they serve. As for those young Punjabi adventurers, Raju Marwari remains in touch with me. His beautiful wife Kajal and three lively children have visited me in Delhi. When I look back at my career of thirty-five years in the Foreign Service, the assistance given to more than 300 illegal Indians to return to their homes was a landmark. It was a singular experience of its kind.

Since the time of being under the Soviet Union, the level of education and training had been very high in Belarus. The teaching of foreign languages, including Hindi, Urdu, and Tamil, was excellent. The same is true for music and ballet. The Music Academy in Minsk has a record of producing some of the best-known international musicians. I was fortunate that one of my Hindi novels was translated into Russian by a Sanskrit scholar, A. Baginskaya (who is one of the finest people I have met), and published in *World Literature* (in the third issue of 1998, edited by Taisa Bondar), which is a magazine in Russian, published from Minsk. As for the Music Academy, I was a regular beneficiary of its performances. Every few months, artists and students of the academy were invited to give recitals at my home to a mixed audience of Belarusian and foreign friends. On one such occasion, the performing artists were relatively young students between the ages of twelve and fifteen years. The music was usually followed by dinner. Keeping the ages of the artists in mind, I purchased soft drinks and juices in large quantities. Gennady, our driver, asked me why I was buying these. When I told him the reason, he smiled politely. After a beautiful performance, when the artists and guests moved towards the drinks and dinner, Gennady requested me to follow him to the room where the drinks were kept. Our young musicians, girls and boys of twelve to fifteen years, were enjoying whiskey with abandon. No one had even looked at a cola or juice. In Russia, they start early, and not just with music.

When the time came to leave Minsk, I was invited for a farewell by the literary association of the city. The invitation was not to the Indian Ambassador, but to a writer. Actually, the reaction of readers of the Russian version of my novel had quite surprised me. It seemed that despite the cultural difference, my story had touched many Belarusians. I had not expected that the farewell organised by members of the literary association would be on such a large scale. Somewhere in the back, I saw the tall figure of Professor Roman, and wondered if he had had a hand in it. What I did not know was that a live TV transmission was relaying the happenings of this function to many more people who were not present there. I came to know of it from my neighbours, an elderly couple who used to share the cherries from their large tree with me, when they came to tell me the next morning that they had been touched by my words at the literary function, and were sorry that I was leaving Minsk.

It is ironic that four years earlier, the news of my posting to Minsk had come as a disappointment. I had requested the Ministry then to post me to any English-speaking place instead of Minsk. However, as I have already recounted, throughout my career, I have never been posted to an English-speaking country. My request had been turned down. I understand that some colleagues who had never done a 'C*' posting and had gone from London to Washington to Paris to Melbourne had complained that I had been given privileged postings in Europe. As it happened, the posting to Minsk, like the posting to Hanoi, turned out to be very special for me.

When the time came to leave Minsk, it was hard. At the airport, I could not hold back my tears. This had never happened to me before.

Notes

1. Following the disputed 2020 Belarusian presidential elections, Lukashenko is facing unprecedented opposition to his rule and has not been recognised as the legitimate President of Belarus by the European Union (EU) or the United States (US). See *BBC News*. 2020. 'Belarus election: Opposition disputes Lukashenko landslide win', 10 August. Available at https://www.bbc.com/news/world-europe-53721410 (accessed September 2021).

Also, see *Euronews*. 2021. 'Revolt, repression and reprisals: A look back at a year of turmoil in Belarus', 9 August. Available at https://www.euronews.com/2021/08/09/revolt-repression-and-reprisals-a-look-back-at-a-year-of-turmoil-in-belarus (accessed September 2021).

2. *The Washington Post*. 2015. 'Don't forget how the Soviet Union saved the world from Hitler', 8 May. Available at https://www.washingtonpost.com/news/worldviews/wp/2015/05/08/dont-forget-how-the-soviet-union-saved-the-world-from-hitler/ (accessed January 2021).

3. A fermented milk drink similar to a thin yoghurt, made by inoculating milk with 'kefir' grains.

4. Since the seventeenth century, the Esterházy Jews were among the great land-owning magnates of the Kingdom of Hungary during the time that it was part of the Habsburg Monarchy, and later Austria-Hungary.

5. The Jama Masjid in Mandu, designed in the Mughal style of architecture, is believed to have been built during the reign of Hoshang Shah, and completed during the reign of Mahmud Khilji in 1454.

10

Lisbon, 2000

A posting as Ambassador to Portugal has something special attached to it. Once one is accredited as Ambassador to Lisbon, one continues to enjoy the privileges attached to the post for the rest of one's life. That is why some prefer to settle in Lisbon after retirement. The biggest attraction is the exemption from paying taxes. So when I got my posting as Ambassador to Portugal, many people asked me if I planned to settle there.

Located on the Atlantic sea front, with an undulating landscape, Lisbon, called Lisboa by its people, is a very attractive and easy-going city. It is the capital of one of the least racist and colour-conscious of European countries. Its population is a mixture of Europe, Asia, Africa, and Latin America. It is a land of poetry and songs. It is perhaps the only country which commemorates the death of one of its most admired poets, Luís de Camões, as its National Day. Fado songs[1] carry with them the echoes of and nostalgia for the time when Portuguese sailors crossed the oceans. Many never returned from those voyages. The sea brought India close to Portugal and with it, the golden age of Portuguese history. The point from which Vasco da Gama sailed for India is situated on a large avenue called 'Avenida da Índia' (Avenue of India). It is hardly 500 metres from the residence of the Indian Ambassador and faces the grand Jerónimos Monastery, an architectural prize of Lisboa. The years of growing trade with India brought unprecedented wealth and exposure to Portugal. It also marked the beginning of the Age of Discovery (fifteenth and sixteenth centuries), when the Portugese capital became the origin of many voyages that would lead to the discovery of Indonesia and other nations as far east as Japan.

The walls of the presidential palace are covered with paintings depicting Indian motifs. At the centre of the large hall where the President receives dignitaries is the painting of an elephant face of Ganesha, surrounded by coconut trees. President Sampaio's wife was from a mixed European and African descent, and is one of the most attractive personalities that I have met. Beautiful, elegant, and composed, it was difficult to take one's eyes off her.

A special feature of Portuguese rule in her various colonies around the world was that Portuguese sailors and settlers were encouraged to marry within the local communities and settle there. The family ties established centuries ago are perhaps the reason for the open-minded attitude towards different races, colours, and religions in Portugal, which strike one as unusual in a European country.

Before taking up my post, it was usual for me to first read the history of the country, and then acquaint myself with the history of its relations with India. The first was done by reading books, and the second was normally found in the files relating to the subject in the Ministry of External Affairs (MEA) in Delhi. In the case of Portugal, I faced a problem in finding sufficient material in the files I could locate in the Ministry. The reason could be the breakup of relations between the two countries in 1961 due to the Annexation of Goa from Portugal by India. There were thirteen years between that break and the resumption of diplomatic relations in 1974. I tried but could find no material in the Ministry on the takeover of Goa in 1961. On reaching Lisboa, I found no material on the subject in the Embassy either. Finally, I sent a request to our Defence Ministry to provide me with their report on the 1961 operation, which ended with Goa being restored to India. A copy of the report was promptly sent to me by diplomatic bag. It surprised me that none of my predecessors, since 1974, had asked for it.

At the time of the takeover of Goa in 1961, Portugal had been under the dictatorship of António de Oliveira Salazar for several decades. This rule had led to the deterioration of the economic and living conditions of its people within the country, and also in its various colonies scattered around in Africa and Asia. Salazar's army had neither the means nor the motivation to hold the country's colonies. Dissatisfaction began growing among the young officers. At the first sign of an Indian army intervention in Goa, the weak and unmotivated Portuguese officers surrendered without the least resistance. There was no fighting, much less any killing. For this easy surrender, the commander of the Portuguese force, Governor General Manuel António Vassalo e Silva (who went against Salazar's orders to prevent the 'useless sacrifice' of lives), was made to pay a heavy price in the form of humiliation meted out to him by Salazar, who held him responsible for the loss of Goa.

The news of the takeover of Goa by force dealt a blow to the international image of Prime Minister Nehru, and the country's claim to be the champion of nonviolence. Within India, the 'armed victory' was treated as a nationalist achievement. Just thirteen years later, at the initiative and involvement of the young officers of the armed forces of Portugal, the country succeeded in overthrowing the autocratic *Estado Novo* (New State) regime (led by Marcello Caetano after Salazar left office in 1968 due to his failing health) in what came to be known as the Carnation Revolution (25 April 1974). It was a peaceful release from a decrepit regime, and a complete disengagement from the overseas colonies of Portugal. One of the prominent leaders of this gentle revolution was Mário Soares, a socialist leader who became the first foreign minister of the new government. That same year, Soares visited Delhi and Goa. Diplomatic relations were resumed between the two countries during that visit. I was then working as Undersecretary in the West Europe division of MEA, and had visited Goa along with the Portuguese delegation. I was quite impressed by the sincere message of Mário Soares that his country was against colonialism, and in favour of self-determination and self-rule. Mário Soares later became Prime Minister, and finally the President of Portugal. For me, my visit with him and his delegation to Goa was an introduction to Goa, which I had not seen before. Actually, I got to know Goa much better many years later, during my time in Lisboa. There I came to know and made friends among the people of Goan origin, which turned out to be one of the most valuable outcomes of my stay there.

In 1974, after the Carnation Revolution, people of Indian origin settled as traders, businessmen, and professionals in the overseas colonies of Portugal had the choice of settling in Portugal. Many Gujarati traders and businessmen from Mozambique chose to move to Portugal. Gujarati Hindu and Muslim businessmen constitute large communities in Portugal. The people of Goan origin, on the other hand, are largely professionals, like doctors, lawyers, engineers, and academics. This community has instituted itself in senior positions in the establishment. The present Prime Minister of Portugal, António Costa, is one of them.

I was initially puzzled to find that the consular department of our Embassy did not treat the people of Goan origin with the same courtesy that was extended to those of Gujarati origin, whether Hindus or Muslims. While the latter group did not have to wait indefinitely to procure visas for travel to India, those from Goa had to do so, sometimes for months on end and even after innumerable visits to the Embassy. Somewhere there was a perception that they had been 'anti-India', if not 'traitors', at some point in the past, which is why they were not deserving of equal treatment. Perhaps the reason was simply because the changed circumstances, after 1974, were not articulated, especially in Goa. Goans continued to be viewed as not being quite faithful citizens of India because they spoke Portuguese and shared a culture with Portugal. Just as no one had seen the report of the takeover of Goa in 1961, the perception vis-à-vis people who were from Goa remained a 'grey' area. Grey areas can very easily turn into prejudices. My first objective was to change this perception. In the process, I came to know and gradually formed friendships with some very fine people, through whom I discovered Goa and its unique cultural heritage. I discovered the Fado songs so special to Portugal, along with discovering the Konkani Mando songs of Goa.[2] Mandovi and Zuari are the two vast rivers which are the life of Goa. The warmth and generosity of some of my friends who have their roots in Goa have remained among the permanent treasures of my years in Lisboa.

One of the first people I called on in Lisbon was Mário Soares. He received me in his private institution, which houses an impressive library and has a think-tank. He was still involved in political discussions and debates, but was now a one-time socialist leader who belonged to the age when equality was valued above development. His son had recently been elected as Mayor of Lisbon.

A unique feature of Portugal is that although its population is largely Catholic, it has offered large tracts of land and funds to people of other religions to build their own places of worship. Hindus and Muslims have received land and funds to build temples and mosques. One of the beautiful monuments on the tourist map of the city is the Ismaili Centre, a mosque designed by Raj Rewal, a leading Delhi architect. A cordial relationship exists between the two Gujarati communities, who participate in each other's public functions. In the year 2002, when large-scale killings in Gujarat became international news, murmurs in the Hindu Gujarati community turned quite loud and one heard comments like, 'Why doesn't the minority community in India make an effort to join the mainstream?' The insinuation was that the violence in Gujarat was due to the minority community's resistance to be like the majority. I found it strange and quite contradictory that a minority (Hindu) group should be voicing such views. This was a strictly vegetarian community living in and as citizens of a nation (Portugal) where the staple food of the majority was fish and meat. Should they be forced to join the majority group's food preferences? The fact is that the social behaviour of the Hindu and Muslim Gujarati communities had nothing in common with the mainstream in Portugal. All marriages are strictly confined within their own communities. Often, brides and grooms are chosen in and come from India. I found it amazing that the Hindu Gujarati community did not see itself as a 'minority' in Portugal, which speaks to the credit of the Portuguese social attitude and its generosity.

Around this time, a very large delegation of the Vishva Hindu Parishad[3] (VHP), an Indian Right-wing Hindu nationalist organisation, visited Lisboa. The leaders of the delegation called on me, and said that the Indian Ambassador should host a dinner for

1,000 people from their delegation and the local Hindu community. I politely informed them that this would go against the secular Indian Constitution. The response of the leader of the delegation was that I should 'expect an appropriate response' to my negative views on their proposal.

The large-scale violence and killings in Gujarat during February 2002 were widely reported in the international media. It was a big blow to the prestige of a country that preached nonviolence. Those of us representing India abroad were left defenceless. To defend the indefensible is a big cross to bear. This had happened once earlier when Prime Minister Indira Gandhi declared Emergency in 1975.

Another unexpected event had suddenly created a lot of commotion for me and my colleagues in the Embassy. Late one night in September 2002, I received a call from the then Chief of the Central Bureau of Investigation (CBI) in Delhi, informing me that a criminal by the name of Abu Salem, who had been absconding, had been arrested by Interpol, along with his girlfriend Monica Bedi, in Portugal. For the CBI, this was a high-priority case because Abu Salem was a prime suspect in the bomb blasts that had taken place in Mumbai in 1993, which had killed many innocent people. This turn of events created circumstances which forced me to get an education in the field of law, which I was least familiar with till then.

The first thing I learnt was that under the existing law of Portugal, a foreigner arrested on criminal charges in his country had to go through the legal process of extradition. There was no provision that allowed him to be handed over to the government of his country without legal clearance from the Portuguese court. In addition, like every member of the European Union (EU), Portugal was under obligation not to extradite a foreign criminal in a case that could end in his being awarded the capital punishment in his country for that offence. I informed the CBI about this. In the meantime, from Indian media reports, it appeared that the CBI was expecting Abu Salem to be handed over to Indian authorities, with the help of the American government. My efforts to convince the CBI and the MEA that Portugal was not a banana republic, and that American 'pressure' should not be expected to change the legal requirements, failed. Within a few days after the arrest of Abu Salem and Monica Bedi, the CBI sent to Lisboa Vijay Shankar, a senior official, to take stock of events concerning this case. Vijay Shankar arrived, along with a very large number of journalists from almost all the big media houses of India, and also from many not so well-known papers and magazines. This was not surprising because the Abu Salem case was 'breaking news' in those days. It was expected that with the assistance of American pressure, Abu Salem was going to be handed over without any further delay. Mr Shankar and the large team of journalists were all prepared to cover this 'Breaking News' at any time. The Portuguese media reported newspaper headlines from Bhopal, where Home Minister L. K. Advani was reported to have said that Abu Salem was going to be brought back to India and would be hanged. Mr Shankar, who later became the head of CBI, had brought to Lisboa a letter from the Home Minister addressed to the Portuguese Foreign Minister, which said that in matters concerning the case of Abu Salem, Vijay Shankar was being deputed to handle consultations with the Portuguese government. The letter was sent to the Foreign Minister.

The next day, I was called for a meeting with the Foreign Minister, who politely told me that our Home Minister's request was not acceptable. He said that the Home Minister's representative cannot replace the Ambassador, because the latter is the representative of the President of India, who is the head of State.

Mr Shankar could not meet the American Ambassador either. Earlier, at a lunch at his home, the American Ambassador in a conversation with me had referred to Abu Salem as 'a small-time gangster'. A senior American intelligence official, who was my neighbour, had expressed his surprise at media reports in India about the American government's interest in Abu Salem. On the other hand, the large contingent of media men and women from India, who followed me in and out of my office, were eager to get the 'breaking news'. Some of these journalists and reporters were staying in the same hotel as Vijay Shankar. One evening, well after 10 PM, I received a call from Mr Shankar. He said that he wanted to share some critical news with me. The CBI had recovered a diary belonging to Abu Salem from his time in Calcutta, in which he had written that he wanted to kill Home Minister L. K. Advani. The next morning, I found the Indian journalists outside my office in a state of excitement. They said that they had 'heard' that I had some critical news.

'Please ask about that news from the source who told you about it,' I suggested to them. The CBI was unhappy with me and complained to the MEA. The Ministry immediately sent Ashok Sharma, who was heading the consular division in Delhi, to Lisbon to ascertain the basis of the CBI's complaint against the Ambassador. I was not acquainted with Ashok Sharma and must admit that his sudden visit gave me an unexpected chance to know a fine officer and an unpretentious person with a keen interest in literature and history. This was also when the CBI and the MEA accepted that there was no option to extradite Abu Salem other than through the process of law. It was also clear that the legal process in Portugal was time-bound and could not be stretched indefinitely for years. I handed over a short list of leading lawyers to Vijay Shankar, from among whom the CBI could make its selection to fight its case in the Portuguese court. I also requested him to meet the lawyers and make the selection. The CBI was disappointed that Abu Salem could not be extradited through an out-of-court settlement. The reason could have been—if not fully, then at least partially—that so far, the CBI had not succeeded in extraditing a single Indian offender from any foreign country. A recent example was that of Octavio Quattrocchi in the famous Bofors case.

Vijay Shankar and the large contingent of Indian journalists left soon after the CBI, somewhat reluctantly, appointed a lawyer for its case. This was followed by a report that appeared in the *Hindustan Times*, which stated that the CBI had not received any support and cooperation from the Indian Ambassador in Lisbon. After this report, I was ready to resign from my post and would have done so had the same paper not published a statement by Ashok Sharma of the MEA contradicting said report. It appears that the MEA had to clear much more than my name; relations between Delhi and Washington needed some deft handling because the American administration was unhappy with loud news reports in the Indian media, often quoting political leaders, that the American administration, even President George W. Bush, was interested in the Abu Salem case.

For me, a new course in legal education began with the filing of the extradition case of Abu Salem by the CBI in the court in Lisbon. Documents translated from Hindi into English were received from the CBI, which were then translated into Portuguese by the Embassy and submitted in court. In the process, around 1,000 documents passed through my hands. I spent several nights reading about cases of extortion and cheating against Abu Salem in Delhi and Mumbai. I patiently waited for the documents relating to his role as the 'prime suspect' in the bomb case in Mumbai of 1993, for which he had been arrested and his extradition sought. No such papers arrived. The crime for which the Home Ministry and the CBI wanted him to be tried, and which had received 'breaking news' coverage in the press, was invisible in the papers that I received.

At the end of 2003, when the case had been fully presented in court, I returned to Delhi on retirement. One evening in 2005, I received a call from the CBI Director, P. C. Sharma. Mr Sharma congratulated me, saying that the judgment of the court in Lisbon had been delivered in favour of the extradition of Abu Salem and Monica Bedi to India, and that he wanted me to be the first to know of this. This was the first extradition case that the CBI had won. Vijay Shankar also spoke to me very appreciatively. The breaking news made headlines. *Hindustan Times* mentioned me in laudatory terms for this achievement in its editorial the next day. Some journalists sought my views and comments, but no one wrote about them.

Monica Bedi was convicted on charges of procuring false passports. She served her term in prison, and has been living a normal life since. Abu Salem has been in Mumbai jail ever since. He has survived in jail because his lawyers had promptly sought special protection for him, which the court had granted right from the beginning. He has been convicted in cases of procuring false passports. Cases of extortion and cheating are still going on against him. As far as I know, no conviction on his role in the Mumbai bomb blast case, in which the Ministry of Home Affairs and the Indian media had announced him as the 'prime suspect', has been made. The media has forgotten this gangster whom they had once raised to the stature of a 'don'.

The Government of India has spent several crores of tax payers' money in nabbing and extraditing him on charges which are yet to be proved. The whole affair resembles a short-lived drama, a sordid form of entertainment. The question which one might still ask is: Why was this particular gangster chosen for the drama that raised a frenzy of emotions among the Indian public? Is it because his name was Abu Salem?

Notes

1. 'Fado' is a genre of music in Lisbon, characterised by mournful tunes and lyrics, about the sea or the life of the poor, coloured by melancholia or *saudade* (symbolising a feeling of irreparable loss and its consequent lifelong damage). The word 'fado' possibly comes from the Latin word *'fatum'*, meaning fate, death or utterance.

2. 'Konkani Mando' is a musical genre which evolved in the nineteenth and twentieth centuries among the Catholics of Goa. This is a confluence of Indian and Western musical traditions, which is often accompanied by dancing and charming ceremonial costumes, with themes such as love mainly, or social injustice and exploitation, or political resistance during the Portugese presence in Goa.

3. Affiliated with the Sangh Parivar, the VHP was classified as a 'religious militant organisation' by the CIA (Central Intelligence Agency of the United States) in 2018.

11

The Right to Information, Delhi, 2004

My involvement with the 'Right to Information' (RTI) movement started many years ago. Aruna Roy, who spearheaded the movement, has been a close friend since our time together at Indraprastha College in Delhi as lecturers. She taught English while my subject was Philosophy. She joined the Indian Administrative Service (IAS) in the same year that I qualified for the Foreign Service. We arrived at the Lal Bahadur Shastri National Academy of Administration in Mussoorie almost together, and were allotted adjacent rooms. This was in July 1968. Some of my best memories of that time, during the foundation course, are of Aruna reading poetry: T. S. Eliot and W. B. Yeats. When in a musical mood, she sang those evergreen songs from the film *My Fair Lady*. We never lost touch. When I returned from my first posting in Vienna, Aruna was posted in Delhi. We spent a lot of time together. I recall that whenever she dropped in on a Sunday and invariably found me experimenting in the kitchen, she would get irritated. The only thing that came in the way of our friendship was my interest in cooking, which she thought was a waste of time.

In 1974, Aruna resigned from service and shifted to Tilonia in Rajasthan where, in the sandy, inhospitable wilderness of Rajasthan, her husband Bunker Roy had the courage to set up an NGO (Non-Governmental Organisation). My father, who had disapproved of Aruna's decision to resign, spent a night in their modest home, which did not have running water. He had gone there to set up a branch of the bank he was working in. On his return, he declared that he thought Aruna had taken the right decision to resign from the IAS, so impressed was he with what he had seen.

Over time, Aruna moved from NGO work to activism. Along with Nikhil Dey and Shanker Singh of their team of MKSS (Mazdoor Kisan Shakti Sangathan), they found large discrepancies while checking the account registers of wages paid to government-contracted labour. In the first place, the wages paid were much less than the minimum wages set up by the government itself. In addition, the lists comprised names of nonexistent workers and others who had been dead for years.

Revelations of downright cheating are possible only if government records are available for public scrutiny. This was the beginning of the movement for the 'Right to Information' in the late 1980s/early 1990s. My friendship with Aruna kept me in close touch with the RTI movement, which I supported even when I was geographically at a distance.

In 2004, when I was settling down in Delhi after retirement, I met Arvind Kejriwal, who was involved along with Aruna, Nikhil, and others in drafting the national Right to Information Act. Arvind, an officer in the Indian Revenue Service, was on long leave from service, and was running 'Parivartan' (*parivartan*, in Hindi, means 'change'), an organisation which helped daily wage earners to acquire ration cards and admission for their children in schools, among other things, through the Delhi Right to Information Act. The Government of Delhi had already passed the RTI Act in 2001, which made it possible for Arvind's organisation to function.

Parivartan had a modest one-room office in a basement in Sundar Nagari, one of East Delhi's poor slums, which has neither sewer lines nor running water. I began by supporting Parivartan and joined their RTI campaigns. These campaigns invariably began with a call: '*Hamaara paisa, hamaara hisaab*' or 'Tax payers' money is our money. It is accountable to us.'

The most dramatic and far-reaching of these campaigns was the 'Right to Water Campaign' (RWC) in 2004–05, which sought information from the DJB or Delhi Jal (water) Board on a reform project that it was planning to launch with the help of the World

Bank. At first, my application for information was turned down by the DJB on the ground that its 'internal matters' were not for public scrutiny, and that there was no World Bank-supported project for privatisation of water distribution at all. However, when I appealed to the Public Grievances Commission, which was the appellate authority, I was, after much resistance, able to get all the papers relating to the World Bank-supported privatisation project from the DJB. What I finally procured was such a mountain of papers that the sheer size filled me with dread. For Arvind, it was a challenge to the expertise he had gained in working for years in the tax office, making sense of what was often intended to be concealed. He immediately set about sifting through the details of the privatisation project.

The documents revealed that in 2002, on the advice of the World Bank, the DJB had commissioned a study on a 'Delhi water supply and sanitation project'. The Bank offered a loan of US$ 2.5 million for the hiring of a consultant by the DJB. After much arm-twisting of the DJB, it got its preferred firm, PricewaterhouseCoopers (PwC), hired as consultant, even though this firm had not been able to clear three of the DJB's evaluations. The Bank forced a change of criterion on the DJB to impose PwC on it as its consultant for the project.

What did PwC propose? First, it silently dropped sanitation or sewage treatment and disposal from the project completely. Private players come for profit, and sanitation work does not provide that. Then it proposed the transfer of twenty-one DJB water zones to private distributors. For appointing private distributors, it fixed criteria which qualified only foreign companies, and kept Indian companies out of the scheme. It proposed that eighty-four management experts (four experts per zone) of foreign companies would draw a salary of $24,400, which is equal to Rs 11,00,000 per month.[1] This meant a rise of Rs 105 crore per annum, or approximately 20 per cent of the total DJB expenditure, implying a proportional water tariff increase for Delhiites. In addition, the private foreign operator would prepare operations budgets annually, for which there was to be no upper limit. If the DJB failed to meet the increased requirement, the private operator would be free of its commitments. Interestingly, the private operator had no responsibility towards augmenting the quantity of available water. Its only task was to receive water, and to distribute it. Providing adequate water remained the task of the DJB.

Suchi Pande of our team carried out detailed research on the work and achievements of foreign private companies engaged in such projects in various parts of the world. The material she unearthed showed that in South Africa, Philippines, and other countries, the water privatisation projects supported by the World Bank had disastrous consequences. As a result, the city of Atlanta in the US (United States) had refused outright to have them conduct a similar project. The most dramatic consequences occurred in Cochabamba, the fourth largest city of Bolivia in South America.

In Cochabamba, a US firm, Bechtel, was given a forty-year contract to privatise water distribution. When it announced a 20 per cent increase in water charges and complete elimination of State subsidies, as ordered by the World Bank, riots broke out in 1999–2000, which led to the private company having to run away. The movement, which threw Bechtel out from Bolivia, mobilised the people to overthrow the government a few years later. At the end of it, public ownership of water was made a law in Bolivia.

A grey area in the project drawn by PwC for DJB was the requirement to reduce leakage of water, or what was called 'non-revenue water'. Slums of Delhi, where a vast population of the city lives, fall into this grey zone of 'leakage'. How this leakage was to be stopped without depriving the slum dwellers of water was not spelt out.

The clandestine approach of the World Bank, and its refusal when we approached it to share the project details with us, showed how hollow its claims about 'transparency' were. Suchi Pande later wrote a succinct piece called 'World Bank Arm-Twisted DJB!', which was published in *Combat Law* in its March–April 2007 issue.

The Right to Water Campaign started with a small group of citizens who shared our concern over Arvind and Suchi's findings, and met in our small apartment. The numbers rapidly increased, making it necessary to find bigger and still bigger meeting places. Along with Aruna Roy and Nikhil Dey and some members of the campaign, Arvind made a presentation on the flawed World Bank-supported water privatisation project at the Delhi Chief Minister's office where the Chief Minister, Sheila Dixit, who was also the chairperson of the DJB, was present along with all the experts and senior members. At the end of the presentation, Mrs Dixit wanted to know details of the experience of water distribution work done by foreign private firms in other countries. No expert of the DJB or the Chief Minister's office had any questions, nor did anyone express doubts about the findings of the study done on information procured through RTI.

Arvind made two more presentations to the Planning Commission. Montek Singh Ahluwalia, then Deputy Chairman of the Commission, was present for the second one. The last straw was a revelation, which also came to light through RTI, that the son of the Deputy Chairman of the Planning Commission had been employed for a period in DJB, even though he was not an expert in water and sanitation matters.

The involvement of a very large number of citizens in this campaign also drew the attention of the print media. Shekhar Gupta of *The Indian Express* recommended that Right to Water Campaign activists should be put behind bars. There were many others like him who also thought that privatisation was the best remedy. A general instinct among elite circles that private companies, especially foreign ones, have the solutions to all problems runs very deep. The Right to Water Campaign proved this inclination to be, at best, a prejudice.

Finally, by the end of 2005, the Government of India felt compelled to withdraw its request for a loan from the World Bank, and scrap the privatisation of the water distribution project drawn by PricewaterhouseCoopers for DJB. This was a very big achievement for RTI, and showed the need for citizen involvement in making governments accountable. However, there was hardly any time to celebrate. Within one year of having passed the national RTI Act in 2005, the government moved to amend the Act in 2006 to deprive it of its teeth.

Resistance to the amendment of the RTI Act was no less than that to the water privatisation project. Activists from outside the capital joined hands. Sandeep Pandey from Lucknow sat on an indefinite hunger strike at Jantar Mantar in Delhi. Anna Hazare sat on an indefinite hunger strike in his village, Ralegan Siddhi, in Maharashtra. Support was extended to the activists by Left political parties, and at the end of about fourteen days of the hunger strikes, the government was compelled to announce the withdrawal of the move to amend the Act.

As I write this in August 2019, the present, newly re-elected NDA-II (National Democratic Alliance, elected in 2019 for a second term) government, which has returned with a massive mandate, has in a sudden move amended the RTI Act without putting it in the public domain, and without allowing people to discuss it, much less to protest against it. The amended RTI Act provides for tight control by the government. The Act has now lost the constitutional authority of a commission like the Election Commission, which it had enjoyed earlier. This is a blow to the work of activists who have been unearthing lapses on the part of public authorities over the past fifteen years.

Among the committed RTI activists is Commodore (Retired) Lokesh Batra,[2] who almost single-handedly unearthed information exposing the casual, near unconcerned handling by the police of what came to be known as the 'Nithari killings'[3] of 2005–06. Many poor children and young women had gone missing in a village called Nithari in Noida, in the adjoining state of Uttar Pradesh on the outskirts of Delhi, and their mutilated body parts were later accidentally discovered in a drain. A rich businessman and his servant have already been convicted[4] in some of the criminal cases of the 'Nithari killings', and are still facing trial in other cases relating to it.

From this period, one of the disturbing incidents that I recall with pain related to a very capable and efficient worker in Arvind's organisation Parivartan. Santosh was a young and spirited RTI worker who became very well-known in the slums of East Delhi. She helped illiterate people get their ration cards and rations. Her popularity among those who benefitted from her efforts was ever on the increase. On some occasions, I accompanied her to ration shops to conduct checks to see that the card-holders were not being deprived of the right quantity and quality of rations. Due to her vigilance, the shopkeepers were unable to get away with diverting subsidised rations into the open market, and thereby making unlawful gains. For them, Santosh was a menace.

In public hearings, which were regularly held in various parts of the city, ration shopkeepers complained that the commission given to them by the government was so inadequate that they had no option but to divert subsidised rations in order to make a living. Santosh was not only an eloquent spokesperson for the ration-card holders at public hearings, but she also encouraged those who were on the receiving end to speak up. On one occasion, she encouraged a poor woman to hand over to Aruna, who was present at the public hearing, a small plastic bag which contained a pinch of grain mixed with dirt and straw, which she had received as ration. A few days later, Arvind and I received a call from the Chief Minister's office saying that Mrs Dixit would like to meet us at her residence that morning. It happened to be Diwali that day. I was perplexed at the urgency. On arrival, we found that along with us, the Secretary of Civil Supplies had also been invited for the meeting.

Mrs Dixit held up the plastic bag with straw and dirt and sought an explanation from the civil supplies' chief official about the quality of ration supplied to the shops. It seemed to me that Aruna, who was a member of the National Advisory Council, must have carried the sample and given it to Sonia Gandhi, Chairperson of the Council, at its recently held meeting. Subsequently, the Delhi government went into action, and started to instal CCTV cameras in and around ration shops.

To return to our star worker Santosh—on two occasions, attempts were made on her life. Santosh was hardly twenty years old. She was walking from her home to Parivartan's office when she was attacked with a knife by someone on a motorcycle. She was taken to hospital in a gravely injured state. That she survived the knife attack on her neck was close to a miracle. This was the second attempt to kill her; the first time, she had ducked and was luckily able to avoid the knife aimed at her throat. We sought a meeting with the Commissioner of Police, which we were able to finally get through the kind intervention of a friend. I was shocked at the indifference with which the Commissioner of Police in Delhi treated our concern for the life of the young worker. He told us casually, while he continued reading a paper called *Star News*, that the matter would be investigated; and then dismissed us by concluding that the process would take time, and that we would be given a report in due course.

No report was ever made or given. The police officer-in-charge at the station later said, when we enquired about the report, that according to their investigation, Santosh had attempted suicide.

Police commissioners have little, if any, interest at all in the happenings in slums. If I had nurtured the illusion that a retired Indian ambassador's concern about a daylight attempt at murder would elicit at least a minimum show of concern from the Commissioner of Police, my hope was shown to be what it was: an illusion.

Finally, in a third attempt on her life, the ration mafia killed her on the road late one evening, when she was driving home on her scooter. By then, RTI activists were either being killed or found dead in mysterious circumstances regularly in all parts of the country. What had begun as a source of inspiration for citizens to seek transparency was turning into a confrontation with entrenched interest groups, be it over land or ration.

I recall that when Santosh returned home from hospital after the second knife attack, her father, who was a tailor, had wept and pleaded that his daughter should not go back to the same work. I was myself so shaken that I tried persuading Santosh to change her line of work. She had laughed at the idea and rejected it. She loved her work and the people of the East Delhi slums loved her. They took turns to look after her and her family during her recovery.

One of the unforeseen aspects of revealing unlawful activity or gains through RTI was that revelations of corruption or naming and shaming do not lead to remedial action on the part of the authorities. I remember obtaining under RTI information from a large private hospital (which had been given free land by the government on its commitment to provide free treatment to poor patients) about the names and addresses of the patients it had treated free of cost. The list I received had the names of the Chief Minister and others like her among those who had been given free treatment. The media is wary of making such information public. It is convenient not to get involved in such matters. As a result, private hospitals are not accountable for any violation of commitments that they have made in exchange for acres of public land free of cost. Delhi's private hospitals are run like five-star hotels only for those who can afford five-star prices. Taking such matters to court requires one to be a lawyer, and to have the time and the means to fight battles in law courts for decades to come. A lot of information that my friends, among them Professor V. P. Srivastav of Delhi University, and I were able to procure under RTI remained only a source of education for us. Most of it could not be used for correcting flaws or for getting justice. The odds are heavily weighted in favour of power and authority, and against RTI activists.

The ultimate blow, however, came later, and was one which none of us had anticipated: Arvind Kejriwal, the leader of the Aam Aadmi Party (AAP), joined all the other political parties in refusing to make available his party's accounts under RTI.[5] Arvind, the RTI activist who had called for '*Hamaara paisa, hamaara hisaab*', who had exposed the flawed privatisation project of the World Bank, did an about-turn when it came to making transparent the accounts of his own party under the RTI Act.

The recent dilution of the RTI Act by the NDA-II government has not come alone. In 2019, after its re-election, the government in its first session of parliament swiftly passed thirty-five bills over thirty-seven sittings,[6] in complete disregard of public opinion. The question of public debate and participation was prevented by not placing the bills in the public domain. The government had congratulated itself on making this the 'most productive' parliament session. However, in this most productive session, it is important to reiterate that not one of the important bills, beginning with RTI,[7] was placed in the public domain. No public discussion preceded their passage. Among them was a bill which deprived Jammu and Kashmir[8] of its existing statehood, abrogated Article 370 of the

Indian Constitution which granted it special status and a degree of autonomy, and also demoted and reorganised Jammu and Kashmir into two Union Territories (UTs) without any discussion with the political leadership and the public of the state, much less their concurrence. Another bill, the Unlawful Activities (Prevention) Act (UAPA),[9] allows the government to declare any individual, even a dissenter, a terrorist at the discretion of the Home Ministry.

The functioning and administration of the government has suddenly changed in a way that distances the public from governance, in the interest of the 'smooth and efficient' running of the government machinery. The bigger question, bigger than the dilution of the RTI, that we face today is: Can democratic functioning, which includes people's participation to the limited extent that has existed so far, possibly return in the near or even the distant future?

The crossroads at which Indian democracy stands today reminds me of a story which our old friend in Vienna, Kazimir Laski, had once related to us. After World War II, a destitute Jew who had survived the Holocaust was advised by a friend to seek assistance from a rich institution, recently set up for that specific purpose. So the poor man took his friend's advice and went to the rich institution. After a long procedure inside, he returned to inform his advisor that he was indeed very impressed by the efficiency and organisation of the institution. The friend asked him, 'So did you get any support?' He shook his head and said, 'No, I got nothing.'

We are today in a similar situation. Efficiency and organisation are being offered in place of people's participation, of which we have been stealthily deprived, in unanticipated moves by the government.

Notes

1. Pande, Suchi. 2007. 'World Bank Arm-twisted DJB!' *Combat Law* March–April: 59.

2. *Fountain Ink*. 2013. 'Nailing the lies of Nithari: How the police and CBI failed the victims of the serial killings', 4 March. Available at https://fountainink.in/reportage/nailing-the-lies-of-nithari (accessed January 2021).

3. *First Post*. 2017. 'CBI court sentences Moninder Pandher, Surendra Koli to death: A timeline of Nithari killings case', 8 December. Available at https://www.firstpost.com/india/cbi-court-sentences-moninder-pandher-surendra-koli-to-death-a-timeline-of-nithari-killings-case-4249187.html (accessed January 2021).

4. In 2017, a CBI special court in Ghaziabad awarded the death sentence to businessman Moninder Singh Pandher and his servant, Surendra Koli, in connection with one of the sixteen murder cases known as the Nithari killings. See *The Hindu*. 2017. 'Koli, Pandher awarded death penalty in Nithari killings case', 8 December. Available at https://www.thehindu.com/news/national/koli-pandher-awarded-death-penalty-in-nithari-killings-case/article21308036.ece (accessed January 2021).

5. See *The Economic Times*. 2014. 'Arvind Kejriwal accused of "running away" from RTI queries on AAP', 25 February. Available at https://economictimes.indiatimes.com/news/economy/policy/arvind-kejriwal-accused-of-running-away-from-rti-queries-on-aap/articleshow/31003693.cms?from=mdr (accessed January 2021).

Also, see *Hindustan Times*. 2014. 'RTI hero Arvind Kejriwal won't share information', 7 February. Available at https://www.hindustantimes.com/india/rti-hero-arvind-kejriwal-won-t-share-information/story-iSUD3hQYqvjOWO4TyV1WUK.html (accessed January 2021).

6. *The Times of India*. 2019. '35 bills passed over 37 sittings: Most productive Lok Sabha session in 20 years', 6 August. Available at https://timesofindia.indiatimes.com/india/lok-sabha-passes-35-bills-over-37-sittings/articleshow/70559976.cms (accessed January 2021).

7. See *The Indian Express*. 2019. 'Explained: What has changed in RTI Act? Why are Opposition parties protesting?', 22 July. Available at https://indianexpress.com/article/explained/what-changes-in-rti-rti-amendment-bill-2019-mean-5840814/(accessed January 2021).

Also, see *India Today*. 2019. 'What makes RTI Amendment Bill so controversial?', 23 July. Available at https://www.indiatoday.in/news-analysis/story/what-makes-rti-amendment-bill-so-controversial-1572596-2019-07-23(accessed January 2021).

8. See *The Hindu*. 2019. 'Explained: How the status of Jammu and Kashmir is being changed', 6 August. Available at https://www.thehindu.com/news/national/other-states/explained-how-the-status-of-jammu-and-kashmir-is-being-changed/article28822866.ece (accessed January 2021).

Also, see *The Telegraph (Online)*. 2019. 'Jammu and Kashmir reorganisation: Reckless assault on federalism and democracy', 5 August. Available at https://www.telegraphindia.com/india/jammu-and-kashmir-reorganisation-reckless-assault-on-federalism-and-democracy/cid/1695920 (accessed January 2021).

Also, see *The Hindu*. 2019. 'J&K loses its special status, divided into two UTs', 6 August. Available at https://www.thehindu.com/news/national/jk-loses-its-special-status-divided-into-two-uts/article28827159.ece (accessed January 2021).

Also, see *The Telegraph (Online)*. 2019. 'Jammu and Kashmir reorganisation: State House nod needed "before" President acts', 5 August. Available at https://www.telegraphindia.com/india/jammu-and-kashmir-reorganisation-state-house-nod-needed-before-president-acts/cid/1695919 (accessed January 2021).

9. *The Wire*. 2019. 'Allowing the State to Designate Someone as a "Terrorist" Without Trial is Dangerous', 2 August. Available at https://thewire.in/rights/uapa-bjp-terrorist-amit-shah-nia (accessed January 2021).

12

Aam Aadmi Party, Delhi, 2012

My short association with the Aam Aadmi Party (AAP) was a bit of a misadventure. It seemed all right at that time to move, almost drift, from a social movement into a political one. In fact, the transition from a civil rights movement into a political party was a big jump. In retrospect, my association with AAP turned out to be a journey to nowhere.

The Right to Information (RTI) movement had, over time, turned into a large public outcry against corruption in government. In 2011, at Arvind's initiative, Anna Hazare came to Delhi to lead the fight against corruption. The target of this movement was the ruling Congress Party. Silently, almost clandestinely, the opposition BJP (Bharatiya Janata Party) succeeded in including some of its front cultural organisations as participants in the movement. A representative of Sri Sri Ravi Shankar's 'Art of Living' foundation became a permanent feature of the leading group around Anna Hazare.

In a misguided move, the government arrested Anna Hazare and Arvind Kejriwal on the day that Anna was to begin his indefinite fast to press the government to legislate a Lokpal Bill (an ombudsman to look into complaints against the government). The arrest brought the entire media and public focus together on the issue of Lokpal. Activists like Medha Patkar (of the 'Narmada Bachao Andolan') and Rajendra Singh (also known as 'Water Gandhi' for having revived dry water bodies and rivers) joined the call for a Lokpal Bill. With each passing day, as septuagenarian Anna became weaker while fasting in public view, support for the movement swelled among the public and the media, with several film stars arriving in Delhi to show their solidarity. Finally, the government succumbed and agreed to talks with Anna and his team on drafting a Lokpal Bill.

The chief organiser of the massive Lokpal agitation was Arvind. Along with Anna Hazare, he became a prominent public figure. On the strength of this success, he decided to form a political party. Anna Hazare was not willing to move from activism to politics. The Right-wing BJP, which had supported the anti-corruption and Lokpal Bill movement, was very much against the formation of what emerged as the Aam Aadmi Party, and put up a resistance to it. However, Arvind Kejriwal and his close associates, Prashant Bhushan and Yogendra Yadav, wanted to strike while the iron was hot. They swiftly moved towards the creation of this new political party on the high tide of success of the anti-corruption Lokpal movement.

Why did I decide to become a founding member of AAP and why was I disillusioned by it just as the party moved towards unprecedented success—won elections and set up a government in Delhi?

It is an undisputed fact that corruption has its roots in the funding of political parties. Money that is given to them is unaccounted for (it is largely this money which has illegally avoided the tax net) and is called black money. The AAP came up promising transparency in political funding. It said that donations to the party would be accepted only through cheque payments, and that the party would display on its website every donation that it received, along with the name of the donor. Like the RTI, this appeared to be a step in the right direction. If political party funding was to become transparent, the power of money in policy-making would also become transparent. No political party before AAP had proposed transparency in fund-raising. It was a 'first time' promise. It stirred my enthusiasm sufficiently for me to join AAP at its formation stage.

The AAP also promised in its Vision Document that tickets to contest elections would be given to candidates chosen by its grass-roots workers/volunteers. These two promises were to distinguish it from all other political parties. A third element that it advertised was that it would abandon the VIP culture. It promised that elected leaders of AAP would live modestly.

In the very first elections it contested for the Delhi Assembly, AAP gave tickets to rejected candidates of the Congress and the BJP, who came with money for their campaigns and also for the party. In some cases, it did so after forcing candidates who had already been fielded with the support of the party's volunteers to withdraw their candidatures in favour of the newcomers. I was dismayed to hear that one of the dedicated AAP members whom I knew from the RTI days had been forced to withdraw her candidature for a newcomer who had been rejected by the Congress party. When I asked Yogendra Yadav about this contradiction with the Vision Document which he had drafted, he politely told me that Arvind was the 'flagship' of the party; therefore, we should not dispute party tickets given at his discretion.

Once it was formed, the party did not call any meeting to discuss political or social issues. Arvind asked me to write a policy paper on issues of foreign policy for the party's election manifesto. I told him that since I did not know the policies of the party, I was not in a position to write about them; he replied that the party would stand by my personal views, whatever they were. This was not a joke. He actually meant it! The same was repeated on the issue of gender justice.

I remember that in the first and only meeting that I attended on writing the party's manifesto, which was headed by Yogendra Yadav, Yadav told me, in response to my question about what the party's ideology was, that it was to tackle every issue and problem, as and when we confront it. In short, it stood for no principles other than the principle of convenience or opportunism. Can a political party do without an ideology, and survive on nothing more than a call for fighting corruption?

As elections approached, tickets were distributed on the principle of convenience, which included how much money a candidate would bring. During election campaigns, khap panchayat[1] chiefs who were known for having ordered the honour killings of young couples were invited to address the party's rallies in Haryana. Anyone who objected to this was told that khap panchayats have culturally strong roots, and are important and traditional organisations that should be given due respect. It is no secret that upper castes, money, and muscle power are in control of khap panchayats. None of these issues—caste, money, and muscle power—was ever discussed among party members. There was no need for discussion. All decisions emanated from the undisputed leader of the party.

When Arvind took oath as Chief Minister of Delhi in front of a sea of supporters, he sang impromptu a Hindi film song on 'fraternal feelings or brotherhood' (*bhaichara*, in Hindi), and seemed to win the hearts of the vast audience before him. He would also ask his audiences to take an oath to neither pay bribes nor accept them. Corruption, to Arvind, meant the illegal transfer of notes from one hand to another. The question of corruption in policy-making was never raised; it was not even considered corruption.

Insiders like myself found out only too soon that the party that was architected to fight corruption was diverging from that vital objective. AAP did not allow RTI to cover it. It still refuses[2] to do so. The question arises: Can a political party survive only on an anti-corruption plank? If anything, AAP is proof of this inadequacy. The promises to abandon VIP culture also seemed to vanish as soon as the Chief Minister and his cabinet colleagues moved into their official residences.

Just a fortnight after the first AAP government was formed, on the intervening night of 15–16 January 2014, Somnath Bharti, a minister in the Kejriwal government, along with a mob of supporters, raided the homes of Ugandan and Nigerian women living in Khirki Extension,[3] a part of his constituency in South Delhi, in the dead of night. The raid was conducted on the mere suspicion that the women were drug addicts and prostitutes. The young women were allegedly beaten, molested, dragged out, humiliated, and forcibly taken to the All India Institute of Medical Sciences (AIIMS), where they were subjected to narcotic tests. All of this was captured, including the objections raised by police officers who were called to the location of the raids, on video cameras by the minister's cronies to be publically displayed as the party's achievement.

The drug tests showed that the women victims of the raid had not[4] taken narcotic drugs. The minister's actions in raiding, humiliating, and forcibly subjecting the women to undergo tests were illegal,[5] and the police officers present had objected to them. The entire late-night drama, where the Aam Aadmi Party's minister and supporters had acted as vigilantes, clearly showed up their racism.

Where was the question of 'fraternity and brotherhood' for African women? They were helpless, few in number, and were not eligible to vote in elections. They were at the mercy of the vigilante workers of the AAP, which was running the government in Delhi.

My criticism of this in the media and within the party elicited no response from the AAP leadership. I wanted to raise the issue in the first general body meeting of the party, which was held just fifteen days later, and proposed that a resolution should be passed, with the consent of the members, offering an apology to the African women who had been humiliated. It should also confirm that AAP was not a racist party. I circulated a draft resolution well in advance of the meeting.

At the meeting, I had hardly spoken three sentences on the subject when Yogendra Yadav, who was presiding over the meeting, snatched the microphone from me and warned me to not 'make a spectacle before the media'. There was no media present. I was heckled and physically forced by party goons to step down and make myself scarce.

All this transpired before 250–300 party members, including Admiral (Retired) Ramdas, who was the Lokpal of the party, its moral guardian. Not a single voice of dissent was allowed to be raised. Absolute loyalty to the party and its leadership was mandatory. That I was allowed to speak even a few sentences was because Admiral Ramdas had firmly stated that he would give his concluding address only after I was given a chance to speak. He had approved of the text of the resolution I had circulated in advance and intended to propose at the meeting.

It was clear not only to me, but also to all the disciplined and loyal members of the party who were present that I was in the wrong place and in the wrong party. Interestingly, I received many telephone calls from party members who were witness to the drama and who voiced their solidarity with me. Some of them, including

Admiral Ramdas and his wife, even took the trouble to visit me the next day.

Amit had told me right in the beginning that he did not think my association with the party would last longer than a year at most. As it turned out, that journey to nowhere, which is how I can describe my association with AAP, was indeed very short-lived.

Notes

1. Khap panchayats are caste or community groups, usually comprising elderly men from the Jat community, prevalent in rural areas of North India, particularly in the states of Haryana, Rajasthan, and Uttar Pradesh. They act as quasi-judicial bodies and often pass regressive diktats, the transgression of which can lead to dire consequences for the youth. See *The Times of India*. 2018. 'Supreme Court declares it illegal for khap panchayats to stall marriage between consenting adults', 27 March. Available at https://timesofindia.indiatimes.com/india/supreme-court-declares-it-illegal-for-khap-panchayats-to-stall-marriage-between-consenting-adults/articleshow/63476839.cms (accessed June 2021).

2. *The Indian Express*. 2014. 'Arvind Kejriwal accused of "running away" from RTI queries on AAP', 25 February. Available at https://indianexpress.com/article/india/india-others/arvind-kejriwal-accused-of-running-away-from-rti-queries-on-aap/(accessed January 2021).

3. *The Hindu*. 2014. 'FIR against "unknown persons" for raid on African women', 19 January. Available at https://www.thehindu.com/news/cities/Delhi/fir-against-unknown-persons-for-raid-on-african-women/article5593899.ece (accessed January 2021).

4. *The Times of India*. 2014. 'AAP minister Somnath Bharti's top 6 controversies', 24 January. Available at https://timesofindia.indiatimes.com/city/delhi/AAP-minister-Somnath-Bhartis-top-6-controversies/articleshow/29286971.cms (accessed January 2021).

5. *Outlook*. 2018. 'Khirki Extension Raid: Molestation Charge Framed Against Somnath Bharti', 17 July. Available at https://www.outlookindia.com/website/story/khirki-extension-raid-delhi-court-frames-charges-of-molestation-against-somnath-/313638(accessed January 2021).

13

Left Behind

In the process of going from place to place, some baggage is often left behind intentionally, but a lot is lost in transit. The heavy baggage which we shed is often a boon to us. Life gets a little uncluttered and is the better for it. The precious and the irretrievable that we leave behind us are our friends, although they accompany us invisibly wherever we go and are never lost. As I reach the end of the lived stories in various parts of the world where I was posted, I have a sense of some other left-behind lived stories which I can share.

I was born at the end of November 1943 in Lahore (undivided India). I would have been about three-and-a-half years old when the city was set in flames, shortly before the Partition. My father, I remember, was trying to reach someone on the telephone, which was dead. All around we saw flames of fire rising. He looked tense and behaved very agitatedly. My elder sister and I stood in front of him. One of us shrieked in terror and received a slap from my father. We both remember the moment, but neither of us can recall who screamed and got the slap.

Like many hundreds and thousands of people fearing for their lives, my parents, along with their three small daughters, moved from Lahore to Delhi. Our grandparents and great-grandfather refused to leave their beloved Lahore, which was 'home'. My father's grandfather died in Lahore on the intervening night of 14–15 August 1947, and had to be cremated within the house, I am told. How my grandparents found their way to Delhi around the end of September, by which time the movement of refugees was almost complete, is another story. Like many hundreds of thousands of refugees, for us too, life was badly disrupted and had to be restarted on uncharted self-made paths.

I was about six or seven years old when the following happened. A Bengali girl named Kajal lived in the house across the street. She was not allowed to come to our house but my younger sister and I often used to go to play with her. One day, we had a fight. I returned home and declared that I would never again go to play with Kajal. By the next evening, I had changed my mind. When I returned from her place, my father asked me, 'So you have made up with Kajal? Which of you said sorry?' To save face, I lied, 'She said sorry.' 'Then she came first. The one who says sorry is always the winner,' my father replied. The prize which was mine had slipped out of my fingers without my knowing it. The regret has remained.

Later, in Queen Mary's School, when I was in class 7, I found my best friend in Neena Bahadur. She opened a new world of many colours for me. Neena was proud of belonging to the original elite Mathur community of Delhi which, during Mughal times, provided the munshis (accountants and officials) to the emperor's office. Their proximity to the rulers led to them adopting the language, cuisine, and refinement of the nobility. In 1857, during what the British called the 'mutiny' and the Indians referred to as the 'First War of Independence', the emperor's accountants supported the British East India Company. As reward, a very large tract of land on the banks of the river Yamuna was later granted to them. The community then moved from their *havelis* (mansions) of Chandni Chowk to large bungalows with gardens on the river front. Neena's family lived in one such house on 16, Yamuna Road. She still lives there in an apartment. More recently, the family has converted that sprawling house and garden into several apartments.

Neena often complained about the horror wrought by refugees from Punjab on the refined culture and life of Delhi. The Punjabis were coarse, she said. I recall her comment that Punjabi women felt no shame in eating *golguppas*[1] standing on the roadside. 'Where do you eat *golguppas*?' I asked her. 'We call the *khonchawala* (peddler) to our home and eat in the privacy of our four walls,' she replied, which quite surprised me. Whenever I returned from her home, my grandmother would ask me what I had eaten at Neena's place. The kebabs and meat preparations at her house were delicious. My grandmother herself was not a Punjabi; although she had married one, she never learnt his language. Her roots were in her beloved Lucknow. As a result, since Punjabi was not my father's mother tongue, we spoke Hindi at home. This is a matter of some regret to me because I missed learning the crisp repartee of Punjabi, which is special to that language. Neena was particularly critical of the way Punjabis addressed their servants with '*tu*',[2] which she said was uncouth. 'Why can't they address them with "*tum*"?'[3] she had asked. Were we really uncouth? It bothered me. I noticed that my grandmother alone used the '*tum*' form and never '*tu*'. It came as a great relief to me when I discovered that the Punjabi language does not have the '*tum*' form. Punjabis were not uncouth, after all. Their language did not allow any other option. But I am not sure that I shared this discovery with Neena. Looking closely at the languages being spoken at home, I noticed that my mother's father, who was a lawyer by profession, spoke in Urdu. It was the language in which he worked. He also wrote and enjoyed Urdu poetry. His wife, my *nani* (maternal grandmother), spoke only Punjabi. The husband and wife spoke to each other in two different languages. My mother spoke to her mother and sisters in Punjabi, but to her brothers and father, she spoke in Hindustani (a mixture of Hindi and Urdu). The brothers spoke to their sisters in Hindustani. Like their father, they did not speak in Punjabi. All this led me to believe that languages have a status. Not all languages are equal.

Neena often parked her bicycle in our house when returning home from school. In course of time, she became very much a part of our teatime. For me, even now, it is a special pleasure to have lunch at Neena's house. The meal is as delicious as it used to be in the old days. Although a lot has changed in the Yamuna Road area since then, it still revives nostalgia in me for those childhood days. The last time I was there, Neena and I had cold beer sitting in her garden. I returned with a beautiful flowerpot in the shape of a bird that she gave me, and which I see before me in my balcony as I write these lines. To Neena, I owe the benefit of learning to see oneself through the eyes of others.

I think I might have been in class 9 when this happened. I had recently read Anne Frank's *The Diary of a Young Girl* (1947), and was discovering other countries through books. One of our classmates, Kalpana Singh, the daughter of the principal of Kirori Mal College, was making other sorts of discoveries and spoke passionately about patriotism. I did not agree with her and said that it was mere chance in which country one is born. If we had been born in Hitler's Germany, our patriotism would have made us Nazis. If we were born in Thailand, our nationalism would have been different. Before I knew it, Kalpana had landed a tight slap on my cheek for my cheekiness in downplaying patriotism. I did not know how to react. So the matter ended there.

Kalpana, like me, did her graduation and postgraduation from Delhi University. I heard that she had married one of her classmates at the university. It was a marriage of her own choice, after which she went to Canada where her husband established a prosperous business. I later came to know that she spent some time in India every year in winter, along with her husband and children. Many years later, I ran into her one evening quite accidentally, while shopping in the market of Safdarjung Development Area. I was then posted at the Ministry in Delhi, and she was here on her yearly visit. Her daughter, about seven or eight years old, was with her. We sat down, the three of us, in a tiny restaurant to catch up over a cup of tea and *pakoras* (a popular Indian snack) and talk about what we had been up to in the time gone by. I cannot remember if I reminded Kalpana of the slap she had landed on me out of her love for patriotism, but it amused me that she was settled in Canada while I was representing my country abroad. Finally, when I asked for the bill and opened my purse, Kalpana's daughter stopped me from paying. When I insisted, she burst into tears. Why, I asked Kalpana, does she insist that her mother should settle the bill? Kalpana explained that the child felt it was unfair that I should pay for the tea and *pakoras* because I belonged to a country of very poor people, while she and her mother were from a very rich country.

I agreed not to pay the bill. The eyes of that child, swimming in tears, touched me deeply. She had turned the slap of patriotism I had received so many years ago into a soft touch of humanism.

When I was studying for my Master's degree in Philosophy at the Arts Faculty in Delhi University, there was a legendary professor by the name of S. K. Bose, whose classes were held at St. Stephen's College. In those days, that college was exclusively for male students. Twice a week in the afternoon, students of Philosophy used to walk to St. Stephen's College for Bose Saheb's class. He was a gentle, small-statured person; a bit of a Bengali Englishman, who had studied at Cambridge University and was passionate about cricket. Those afternoons when interesting cricket matches were held, Bose Saheb could be seen watching cricket, and we knew that he would not hold his class. His students took him very seriously. He taught us the idealist philosophers, and we took down every word that he uttered. In some context, he mentioned a philosopher by the name of F. H. Bradley and his book called *Appearance and Reality* (1893). I went straight to the library to find it. Find it I did, the largest of large books, but its content was well above my understanding. I grappled with it for several days, but without any success. Disheartened, I came to the conclusion that philosophy was not the right subject for me. I should change to a study of Hindi literature. I said so to Bose Saheb very frankly, emphasising that I could not move beyond page 18 of Bradley's *Appearance and Reality*. He looked delighted instead of concerned, and said, 'A very healthy sign!' I thought that he had perhaps not heard me correctly, so I repeated it again, this time louder. He in turn repeated 'a very healthy sign', much louder this time. I was puzzled and told him that I was going to change from philosophy to Hindi literature. He shook his head and said, 'No, philosophy is your subject. Not many admit that they do not understand. Don't give up philosophy.' I took him seriously and have no regrets.

At one stage, I was offered admission to study philosophy in both the universities of Oxford and Cambridge in the United Kingdom (UK). I sought Bose Saheb's advice on which of the two was better. He looked at me curiously and asked, 'Don't you have a non-rational reason to make your choice?' The non-rational reason finally took me in a different direction. It led to my taking the competitive examination through which I joined the Indian Foreign Service. When at a crossroads, I have found Bose Saheb's words about non-rational choice helpfully coming back to me.

When teaching Spinoza's philosophy, he suggested that it might be easier to understand this great idealist philosopher better if we read his biography first. In fact, with hindsight, I think this is true of most thinkers. Their life often reflects much more than their words do. In the case of existentialist thinkers, some of them are best understood through their novels and plays. I thought Jean-Paul Sartre's big treatise, called *Being and Nothingness* (1943), fell into the same category as Bradley's *Appearance and Reality*. I complained to Professor Margaret Chatterjee of the Philosophy department at Delhi University that Sartre's book, which was a prescribed text in our course, made little sense to me. Her response came the next day, which happened to be a Sunday. She telephoned me early in the morning and suggested that I should go and see a morning show of the film called *The Condemned of Altona* (1962), which was showing at reduced rate at a cinema hall I was unfamiliar with. Along with my younger sister Sudha, I set out to find Race Course Cinema. We both sat through the film, which was based on the play of the same name by Sartre. It certainly made more sense than the writer's book prescribed for our course. But the unforgettable part of the experience was the presence of innumerable rats in the cinema hall. Sudha and I sat with our legs curled under us to escape them. The audience comprised largely of people who did not understand English. Not a word of it. They had probably been lured by the reduced rates of the show, and the prospect of sitting under fans on a sweltering summer morning.

It is through the plays of Sartre and the novels of Albert Camus that existentialism not only made sense to me, but it actually became and remains my most preferred school of philosophy. Philosophy and literature, I found, are very close to each other. A lot that cannot be said in words can be grasped better through plays and poetry, and of course, stories.

❖

Several years later, when I was posted as Ambassador in Minsk, a series of events starting with a bit of a traumatic jolt turned into a strange experience. In the autumn of 1997, the University of Bologna in Italy was celebrating its 900th anniversary. Some prominent Indian professors were invited to the celebrations of the oldest European university. Amit was among the invitees, and we planned to meet in Rome before this event. He was also going to lecture in Naples, after which we were to go together to Bologna. Naples is a captivating place. Our taxi driver tempted us to go to Pompeii, and then drove us to a traffic signal. Suddenly, the taxi door on my side opened and a young man tore my handbag from my hands and disappeared as swiftly as he had appeared. In the course of this short operation, he had dealt a heavy blow to my legs, which I later found were bruised badly. We reported the matter to the police. This part of Italy is known for being under the complete control of mafia gangs. I had lost not only money, tickets, keys, and credit cards, but also my passport. The driver, as he dropped us at the railway station, said to me, 'Madam, you are lucky you were not shot dead. Thank your stars that you are alive.'

I was lucky that I could get a duplicate passport the next day in Rome. With that in hand, we could travel to Bologna. The trip by train from Rome to Bologna was complicated because, after taking our seats in the compartment, Amit went to get some sandwiches. He had been at the university and had had no time for lunch. In the process, he missed the train. I found myself without a handbag and without tickets for this train journey, and without any money. The baggage was with me on the train. What was most reassuring was that when the ticket check was made, all the passengers supported me in saying that they had seen Amit, and that he had missed the train. I was worried that Amit had boarded the wrong train, and might end up in Naples instead of Bologna. The age of mobile phones had not quite caught up, so a lot was left to one's imagination. As evening turned into night, I began to wonder what I would do on arriving in Bologna. Without any money, I could not find a hotel. I did have my passport in my overcoat pocket. I would have to go to the police station, show my passport, and say that I was the Ambassador of my country. The likelihood was that no one would believe me. The passport had been issued that very day, it had no stamp of arrival in Italy. The next morning, the newspapers would have the pleasure of reporting that a mad, penniless Indian woman had come with a false diplomatic passport, declaring herself to be the Ambassador of her country. The idea was so funny that I could not help laughing. When the train arrived at Bologna station, all the passengers helped me take down the baggage. They asked me if I needed any help. Before I could request to be taken to the police station, I saw a tall princely figure approaching me. The sight of Massimo Ricottilli was such a relief that the burden which I had been carrying through the journey just slipped off my shoulder. He was smiling. A professor at the University of Bologna, Massimo was Amit's friend from his college days in Cambridge. His wife had received a telephone call from Amit informing her of my plight, so Massimo was there to take me to the hotel, after which he took me out for dinner. It was a wonderful dinner and Massimo, who is a wine connoisseur, chose the best wine for the occasion. At the hotel, there was some confusion because my passport had no arrival stamp and had been issued that very morning. Amit arrived halfway through our dinner. He had not taken the train to Naples after all, thank heavens for small mercies.

At the inauguration of the celebrations at the university the next morning, among others, we met our friend Romila Thapar, the distinguished Indian historian. Later in the evening, while walking around the old city, we went into a large bookstore where, while looking around, Romila's wallet was stolen from inside her handbag. She lost all her money. I had intended to go to the market that day to buy a handbag. So with a vague idea about where we could buy our requirements, Romila and I walked towards a market and got lost. At one point, we saw two middle-aged ladies whom we approached to ask for directions. As we went near them, they appeared scared at the sight of two sari-clad women and quickly turned and ran from us. 'They thought we were Romanian gypsies,' I told Romila. The Romani[4] people are seen as an outcast people who wear long skirts, are a little darker in colour, and beg to make a living. They are feared as pickpockets and robbers. Romila was horrified at the thought that we, yes we, including a most distinguished professor like her, could have been mistaken for Romanian gypsies. I was quite amused at the thought that while it was Romila and I who had been robbed clean, we were the ones taken to be robbers!

I could not help laughing at how perceptions can be so far removed from reality. At the drop of a hat, even the distinguished can be placed on the receiving end of prejudices. Those who have been robbed are seen as robbers. Such is life.

It was the summer of 1975. We were in Calcutta when we received an invitation to lunch from the British Consul General there. Sir John Hicks, a British economist, was on a visit to India and wanted to meet Amit. Hicks had just received the Nobel Prize in economics (1972). As it happened, there were only four guests at the lunch, the Hickses and us. At the table, I was sitting between Professor Hicks and the wife of the Consul General. She was a pleasant person, and in reply to my question said that of all the places where her husband had been posted, she had enjoyed most the years they spent in Lahore. One of her daughters had been born there. I told her that I was born in Lahore, and wanted some day to visit the city for which my parents and grandparents still carried nostalgic memories. She said that she had loved the house they lived in. Its veranda overlooked the racecourse, it had large palm trees—it was a world by itself. I remembered it so well. One of my first memories is of standing on that large veranda on the first floor—a parrot called Mithu hanging in a cage, the palm trees outside, and my great-grandfather walking up the stairs. I could hardly breathe, much less swallow my food, as she spoke about our house, which had also been hers. Reliving the memory which she had evoked in me was a very emotive experience.

The fact is that my grandfather had left his house at Racecourse Road on a caretaker basis with the British representative in Lahore. He never thought that he was leaving Lahore for good. He did return later, many times, but as a visitor with diminishing hopes of ever going back to his roots.

Papa ji, as we called him, was a prominent member of the Punjab Chamber of Commerce. He had several factories in West Punjab. In early 1947, he, along with his confederates, received a delegation of the Indian National Congress led by Jawaharlal Nehru. The latter informed them about the imminent partition of the country, and that very soon Lahore was going to be part of Pakistan. He strongly advised that industries and assets be shifted to East Punjab or Delhi. Machines should be dumped, if necessary, on the roads of Amritsar, which was only 30 miles away. While others pondered, some took to shifting immediately, but *Papa ji* thought that it was 'absurd' to leave one's home because of political changes. His two brothers decided to leave Lahore and shifted to Saharanpur, where they had a factory. His sons tried to persuade him, but could not change his mind. My father, who was the elder son, finally shifted his own family to Simla in the care of a relative there, and went to look for a job and a roof in Delhi. Lahore went through burning, killing, and fleeing. *Papa ji* stayed on in Lahore, convinced that the madness would end sooner rather than later. He had many friends, and among them were some prominent members of the Muslim League, including Liaquat Ali Khan, who became the first Prime Minister of Pakistan.

On the night of 14–15 August 1947, when Pakistan and India were celebrating their respective independence, *Papa ji*'s father, who had also refused to leave Lahore, died very suddenly. The situation in the city was such that he had to be cremated in the garden of the house. Some of the wooden doors of the house were used for the funeral pyre. By this time, there were hardly any Hindu families left in Lahore. *Papa ji* believed that gradually, things would return to normal for those few like him who were living within closed doors and windows. In mid-September, he received a phone call from his friend Liaquat Ali who said that, according to intelligence reports, *Papa ji* and his wife's lives were in danger, and that he wanted to guarantee a safe passage on a private plane for his friend and his wife to Delhi in the next few hours. That gave *Papa ji* and *Bari-mummy* just enough time to gather what they could in a suitcase, and to leave for the airport in the official car of the Prime Minister along with his motorcycle escort. Along with them were *Papa ji*'s trusted servant Jagat Ram (who stayed with him till the end) and Devi, his gardener, who also travelled to Delhi by the same plane, as did the parrot Mithu.

Papa ji visited Lahore several times in the next few years, and always stayed with his trusted friends. On one such visit, he left his house on a caretaker basis with the British representative in Lahore.

Papa ji's friend, Liaquat Ali Khan, was assassinated in 1951. But till early 1965, *Papa ji* went to Lahore many times. Some family friends from Lahore also visited us in Delhi. Of those visits, I have clear memories of much warmth and laughter. Religion did not destroy friendships. What destroyed those bonds was the 1965 war between India and Pakistan. That destroyed forever the possibility of friends crossing the border to meet, greet, share, and laugh with each other. It was then that the personal became political.

Notes

1. *Golguppas* are a popular Indian snack and common street food.

2. In Hindi, '*tu*' or the informal, intimate 'you' can also be read as the abusive, demeaning 'you'.

3. In Hindi, '*tum*' is the more formal 'you', yet it is less dignified than '*aap*'.

4. The Romani people are a traditionally itinerant, Indo-Aryan ethnic group who have originated from the Indian subcontinent, and live mostly in Europe and the Americas as diaspora populations. It is important to distinguish between the Romani people and the Romanians (people of the country, Romania). However, the Romani people do constitute one of Romania's largest groups of minorities (this group is referred to in the text as 'Romanian gypsies').

A Significant Judgment

The Supreme Court Judgment of 1979 which denounced gender discrimination in the IFS.

IN THE SUPREME COURT OF INDIA

ORIGINAL ~~APPELLATE~~ JURISDICTION

WRIT PETITION NO. 743 OF 1979

Miss C.B. Muthamma, I.F.S.	Petitioner
Vs.	
The Union of India & Ors.	Respondents.

J U D G E M E N T

KRISHNA IYER, J.

This writ petition by Miss Muthamma, a senior member of the Indian Foreign Service, be speaks a story which makes wonder whether Articles 14 and 16 belong to myth or reality. The credibility of constitutional mandates shall not be shaken by governmental action or inaction but it is the effect of the grievance of Miss Muthamma that sex p-rejudice against Indian womanhood pervades the service rules even a third of a century after Freedom. There is some basis for the charge of bias in the rules and this makes the ominous indifference of the executive to bring about the banishment of discrimination in the heritage of service rules. If high officials lose hopes of equal justice under the rules, the legal lot of the little Indian, already priced out of the expensive judicial market, is best left to guess. This d-isturbing thought induces us to make a few observations about the two impuged rules which appear, prima facie, discriminatory against the female of the species in public service and have surprisingly survived so long, presumably, because

..,2

- 2 -

servants of government are afraid to challenge unconstitutional rule making by the Administration.

Miss Muthamma, the Petitioner complains that she had been denied promotion to Grade I of the Indian Foreign Service illegally and unconstitutionally. She bewailed that, to quote her own words :

> ".... one of the reasons for the petitioner's suppersession is the long standing practice of hostile discrimination against women. Even at the very threshold when the petitioner qualified for the Union Public Services at the time of her interview, the Chairman of the U.P.S.C. tried to persuade (dissuade ?) the petitioner from joining the Foreign Service. On subsequent occasion he personally informed the Petitioner that he had used his influence as Chairman to give minimum marks in the viva. At the time of entry into the Foreign Service, the petitioner had also to give an underta-king that if she were to get married she would resign from the service.
>
> That on numerous occasions the petitioner had to face the consequences of being a woman and thus suffered discrimination though the Constitution specifically under Article 15 prohibits discrimination on grounds of religion, race, caste, sex or place of birth and Article 14 of the Constitution provides the principles of euqlity beforelaw ....
>
> That members of the Appointments Committee of the Union Cabinet and the respondent No. 2 are bascially prejudiced against women as a group. The Prime Minister of India has been reported in the Press as having stated - it will not be irrelevant here to mention that most of the women who are in the service at senior levels are being very systematically selected for posts which have traditionally been assigned a very low priority by the Ministry."

If a fragment of these assertions were true, unconstitutionality is writ large in the administrative psyche and masculine hubris which is the anathema, for part III haunts the echelons in the concerned Ministry. If there be such gender

....3

- 3 -

injustice in action, it deserves scrupulous attention from the summit so as to obliterate such tendency.

What is more manifest as misogynist in the Foreign Service is the persistence of two rules which have been extracted in 4 the petition. Rules 8(2) of the Indian Foreign Service (Conduct & Discipline) Rules, 1961, unblushingly reads :

> "Rule 8(2) : In cases where sub-rule (1) does not apply, a woman member of the service shall obtain the permission of the Govt. in writing before her marriage is solemnised. At any time after the marriage, a woman mem-ber of the Service may be required to resign from service, if the Govt. is satisfied that her family and domestic commitments are likely to come in the way of the due and efficient discharge of her duties as a member of the service."

Discrimination against women, is traumatic transparency, is found in this rule. If a woman member shall obtain the permission of government before she marries, the same risk is run by government if a male member contracts a marriage. If the family and domestic commitments of a woman member of the Service is likely to come in the way of efficient discharge of duties, a similar situation may well arise in the case of a male member. In these days of nuclear familis, inter-continental marriages and unconventional behaviour, one fails to understand the naked bias against the gentler of the species. Rule 18 of the Indian Foreign Service (Recruitment, Cadre, Seniority and Promiton) Rules 1961, runs in the same prejudicial strain :

> "(1) ....
> (2) ....
> (3) ....
> (4) No married woman shall be entitled as of right to be appointed to the service."

...4

- 4 -

At the first blush this rule is in defiance of Article 16. If a married man has a right, a married woman, other things being equal, stands on no worse footing. This misogynous posture is a hangover of the masculine culture of manacling the weaker sex forgetting how our struggle for national freedom was also a battle against woman's thraldom. Freedom is indivisible, so is Justice. That our founding faith enshrined in Articles 14 and 16 should have been tragically ignored vis-a-vis half of India's humanity, viz our women, is a said reflection on the distance between Constitution in the book and Law in action. And if the Executive, as the surrogate of Parliament, makes rules in the teeth of Part III, especially when high political office, even diplomatic assignment, has been filled by women, the inference of die-hard allergy to gender parity is inevitable.

We do not mean to univarsalise or dogmatise that men and women are equal in all occupations and all situations and do not exclude the need to pragmatise where the requirements of particular employment, the sensitivities of sex or the peculiarities of societal sectors or the handicaps of either sex may compel selectivity. But save where the differenti-ation is demonstrable, the rule of equality must govern. This creed of our Constitution has at last told on our governmental mentation, perhap-s partly pressured by the pendency of this very writ petition. In the counter affidavit, it is stated that Rule 18(4) (referred to earlier), has been deleted on November 12, 1973. And, likewise, the Central Government's affidavit avers that Rule 8(2) is on its way to oblivion since its deletion is being gazetted. Better late

....5

- 5 -

than never. At any rate, we are in relieved of the need to
scrutinise or strike down these rules.

The p-etitioner has, after the institution of the proceeding
been promoted. Is it a case of post hoc ergo propter hoc ?
Where justice has been done, further probe is ofiose. The
Central Government states that although the petitioner was not
found meritorious enough for promotion some months ago, she
has now been found to be good now, has been upgraded and
appointed as Ambassador of India to the Hague, for what it is
worth. Her surviving grievance is only one. During the interval
of some months between her first evaluation and the second,
some officers junior to her have gone above her. In the rat
race of Indian official life, seniority appears to be acquiring
a religious reverence. Since the career ahead of the petitioner
may well be affected by the factum of prior birth into Grade I
of the Service, her grievance turning on senioritycannot
be brushed aside. Her case, with particular focus on seniority,
deserves review vis-a-vis those junior to her who have been
promoted in the interval of some months. The sense of injustice
rankles and should be obliterated so that every servant in
strategic position gives of his or her best to the country.
We have had the advantage of the presence of the learned
Solicitor-General, appearing for the Union of India, With
characteristic fairness he has persuaded his clientbto agree to
what we regard as a just gesture, viz., that the Respondent-
Union of India will shortly review the seniority of the
petitioner, her merit having been discovered and her seniority
in Grade II being recognised. We direct accordingly.

...6

- 6 -

Subject to what we have said above, we do not think it necessary to examine the averments of mm mala fides made in the petition. What we do wish to impress upon Government is the need xf to overhaul all Service Rules to remove the stain of sex discrimination, without waiting for ad hoc inspiration from writ petitions or gender charity.

We dismiss the Petition but not the problem.

Sd/-
...........................L.
(V.R. KRISHNA IYER)

Sd/-
...........................J.
(P.N. SHINGHAL)

New Delhi
September 16, 1979.

A Few Photographs

PHOTOGRAPH 1: Author with the group that staged *Abhigyan Shakuntalam*, Vilnius, 1998.

Note: The author is in the last row (fourth from left) with the director of the play on her left. The consular assistant to the author at the Indian Embassy in Minsk then, V. Radha is kneeling in a sari in the bottom row.

Source: V. Radha's collection.

PHOTOGRAPH 2: Raju Marwari, a rescued illegal immigrant in Minsk.

Source: A screenshot from *Road to Germany* (1997), a documentary film by Jogendra Bhagat, the consular assistant to the author at the Indian Embassy in Minsk at the time.

PHOTOGRAPH 3: Jogendra Bhagat (right) with one of the survivors of the container which had overturned (this young man had lost his teeth).

Source: A screenshot from *Road to Germany* (1997).